# THE LAWS OF
# MISSION

## ESSENTIAL TRUTHS
## FOR SPIRITUAL AWAKENING
## IN A SECULAR AGE

## RYUHO OKAWA

IRH PRESS

BOOKS
IRH PRESS
New York

Library of Congress Cataloging-in-Publication Data

ISBN 13: 978-1-942125-24-2
ISBN 10: 1-942125-24-0


Printed in Canada


First Edition


Book Design: Whitney Cookman
Cover image: © Shutterstock / A. and I. Kruk

# Contents

Contemplative Quotes I:
Awaken to the World of Truth

CHAPTER ONE
# Living in the Age of the Mind
The Power of the Mind that Will Create a Golden Life

CHAPTER TWO
# How to Become an Attractive Person
### The Power to Turn Critics into Fans

Contemplative Quotes II:
What is Missionary Work?

CHAPTER THREE

# The Starting Point for Human Happiness
The Importance of Faith and a Religious Mind

Contemplative Quotes III:
As Long as You Have Faith as Thin as a Spider's Thread

CHAPTER FOUR

# The Power of Miracles To Change the Era

Religion and Politics that Can Overcome the Era of Crisis

CHAPTER FIVE
# Awakening to the Power of Mercy
May Love Reach the Hearts of Many

Contemplative Quotes IV:
The Difference between Terrorism and Revolution

CHAPTER SIX

# To the World We Can Believe In

You, Too, Have the Light to Bring Happiness to the World

**1. Changing the World Through the Revolution of Happiness**

**2. To Live in the World We Can Believe In**

**3. Faith is Something You Embrace and Feel with All Your Heart and Soul**

**4. Your Ultimate Goal is to Completely Believe in God**

Contemplative Quotes V:
Everything Becomes Light When We Break Through Walls

Afterword • 209

# PUBLISHER'S INTRODUCTION

For the past thirty years, Ryuho Okawa, Japanese spiritual, religious, political, business, economic and educational visionary and best-selling author of over 2,200 books and over 100 million copies of these books sold worldwide [translated into 28 languages], has published an annual volume of the core of his teachings which has come to be known internationally as the "Laws Series." *The Laws of Mission: Essential Truths for Spiritual Awakening in a Secular Age* is the latest and the 23rd of the Laws Series, which is a compilation of six of the lectures that Okawa delivered to a wide range of audiences in various locations around Japan from 2013 to 2016. In this book, Okawa provides answers to questions about life and death, the soul and mind, as well as solutions for issues on a global scale, such as religious conflicts, political and economic problems, and an increasing influence of materialism and atheism.

In this day and age of advanced scientific and information technology, we are often deluded by a false sense that we know everything. But in fact, many people cannot even answer simple but fundamental questions about life such as, "What's the purpose of our life?" and "What happens after death?" In *The Laws of Mission*, Ryuho Okawa offers integral spiritual truths that bring about spiritual awakening within each of us. This book helps us find the purpose and meaning of our life and make the right decisions so that we can walk the path to happiness.

## Global Visionary Ryuho Okawa

Ryuho Okawa is recognized internationally as a global visionary, thinker, author, as well as a spiritual leader. In 1986, Okawa, after working for an international trading firm and gaining experience in the United States, founded Happy Science as a spiritual movement. It is dedicated to bringing greater happiness to humankind by uniting religions and cultures to live in harmony and by overcoming various barriers among humanity. Happy Science has grown rapidly from its beginning in Japan to a worldwide organization. Today it has 12 million members around the globe with branches in New York, Los Angeles, San Francisco, Tokyo, London, Sydney, Sao Paulo, and Hong Kong, among many other major cities. This global movement is leading the future of the world—having impact on enlightening individuals, religious organizations, and governments with help of a new vibrant political party in Japan, Happiness Realization Party. Ryuho Okawa has dedicated his life to the exploration of the Truths, and he continues to address large gatherings throughout the world, having given more than 2,600 lectures and through live broadcasts and TV programs. He also established Happy Science Academy Junior and Senior High schools and Happy Science University.

Most recently in the United States, Ryuho Okawa delivered an extraordinary speech, "Freedom, Justice, and Happiness" in New York City in October 2016. His teachings continue to spread throughout North America today. Okawa's books including *The Laws of the Sun*, *The Laws of Justice*, *The Laws of Success*, *Invitation* to Happiness, *Think Big!*, *The Heart of Work*, *The Essence of Buddha*, *The Miracle of Meditation*, *A Life of Triumph*, *The Unhappiness Syndrome*, *Healing from Within*, and *Invincible Thinking* are all now carried throughout the United States in Barnes & Noble stores as well as independent and leading online retail bookstores. Okawa was also featured in an eight-part television show on the Fox affiliate, WNYW-TV FOX 5 in New York and in advertorial features in *The Economist*, *The National Review*, and *The Weekly Standard*.

## Lectures put together in a "live" style for readers

*The Laws of Mission* is a series of transcripts of Okawa's live lectures that were put together in a style that lets readers experience a sensation of actually being there as Okawa speaks from a variety of angles, addressing topics that cater to the audience and the state of society. The book also includes five Contemplative Quotes, between chapters, to help readers deepen their understanding of the theme of the book.

*The Laws of Mission* begins with **Chapter 1 "Living in the Age of the Mind"** which was Okawa's lecture given to an audience at a Happy Science local temple located in Tachikawa City, Tokyo. In this chapter, Okawa stresses the importance of knowing that our life does not end at the time of death. How will our life in this world change when we become aware of the truth that we can take with us experiences we gain in this world even after we become souls in the other world? How can we as individuals use the power of our mind to create our future? Okawa offers answers to these questions to the audience in a friendly manner.

**Chapter 2 "How to Become an Attractive Person"** is Okawa's lecture given to an audience of about 1,000 in the prayer hall of Happy Science Tokyo Shoshinkan. He shares the lessons he learned through his real-life experiences including his time at an international trading firm, while discussing ways to overcome adversities and setbacks and the essentials to becoming a leader. This chapter will help us find hints to overcome jealousy and an inferiority complex and transform these negative thoughts into the source of positive energy.

**Chapter 3 "The Starting Point for Human Happiness"** is Okawa's seminar given in his birthplace, Tokushima Prefecture, to an audience of about 5,000 in the year 2016, the 30th anniversary of the founding of Happy Science. Okawa explains in a simple manner, that the starting point of Happy Science's aim is to bring happiness to humankind and that there are two stages of enlightenment we must awaken to during our life on earth. In addition, he talks about political issues from the perspective of a religious leader by referring to the Kumamoto earthquake that occurred one week before the lecture.

**Chapter 4 "The Power of Miracles to Change the Era"** is Okawa's earnest message to an audience of about 9,000 in Fukuoka, a city in Western part of Japan, in March 2016. He has published over 400 titles of spiritual messages for the last 30 years since the founding of Happy Science in an effort to prove the existence of the spiritual world, and in this chapter, he uncovers the true meaning of natural disasters, the truth he discovered through spiritual messages he received from heaven. Okawa also reveals underlying truths behind the tensions in the Asian region around the time of the lecture. Moreover, he offers a spiritual perspective on the political direction Japan should take in its national defense policies, and the role religions should play in solving conflicts among different beliefs and in creating a world of peace and harmony.

**Chapter 5 "Awakening to the Power of Mercy"** is a lecture Okawa gave in Sendai, a city hit by the Great East Japan Earthquake, at a Happy Science temple built in 2012, the year following the earthquake, to serve as a lighthouse to save the souls of victims and provide comfort to survivors. If God is a merciful being, why do people continue to suffer religious conflicts between Islam and Christianity? How can we overcome hatred and violence among different religions? This chapter will help us gain a deeper understanding of the power of mercy that every person in the world needs to awaken to today.

**The final chapter, "To the World We Can Believe In,"** is a lecture by Okawa given to an audience of 7,000 people at the El Cantare Celebration in Makuhari Messe, a huge international exhibition hall, Chiba Prefecture, in December 2015. The El Cantare Celebration is one of the major annual events of Happy Science. The lecture was broadcast to 4,000 satellite locations throughout Japan and the world. This chapter mentions a spiritual being named El

Cantare, who has been guiding all world religions with the goal of bringing happiness to the entire humankind. Okawa sees a need to bring about "the Revolution of Happiness" based on the new and all-encompassing Truths that are taught in the present era. He refers to the 2014 American movie *God's Not Dead* to show what the ideal relationship between the academics and religions should be. He then casts light on how we can turn this world into the world we can believe in, which is the main theme of this chapter.

As the publisher of this book, we sincerely pray that the ideas in this book will go beyond academic studies and spread far and wide, and bring happiness and peace to the world.

# PREFACE

Few people are aware that

They are now living in a time of Light.

This is because the world is full

Of various kinds of disasters and misfortune.

However, that is why I tell you this.

"Now is the time."

When humanity is suffering in the depths of agony,

God, too, is there.

Here, I preach *The Laws of Mission*.

While they are the Laws of Salvation,

They are also the Laws of Love,

The Laws of Forgiveness,

And the Laws of Truth.

Here are the answers to your questions.

Bore a tunnel through the mountain of agnosticism.

*Ryuho Okawa*
*Founder and CEO of Happy Science Group*
*December 2016*

# AWAKEN TO THE WORLD OF TRUTH

*This world is the exact opposite*
*When seen from the world of truth.*
*This world that you see with your eyes*
*Is just like what you see*
*On the surface of a pond,*
*Where you think*
*That the mirrored image of yourself*
*Is your true self.*
*The world you see is not the real one.*
*It is just a world*
*Reflected on the pond before you.*

*To put it differently,*
*The world you believe to be real and true*
*Is just a shadow*
*Imitating and reflecting the world of truth.*
*You must know this.*

*You may not believe that*
*Movie scenes are real when you watch them;*
*In the eyes of those in the spiritual world,*
*Or the true world,*
*Who are watching you living in this world,*
*Your life in school or in society*
*Is like a movie.*
*Although the world in which you live*
*Is the fictional world that imitates reality,*
*The fictional world is the very world*
*In which you live.*

*The world that you believe is real*
*Is not the world of truth.*
*The one you think is fantasy,*
*The world you have only heard of*
*In myths, legends and religions*
*Is the true world.*

From *How to Become an Awakened One*

# Chapter ONE

# Living in the Age of the Mind

*The Power of the Mind that Will
Create a Golden Life*

# 1

# Modern-Day Society No Longer Understands the Meaning of the Mind

✧　　✧　　✧

### *Commonly accepted knowledge nowadays says*
### *That the mind is a part of the brain*

This chapter entitled, "Living in the Age of the Mind," deals with a topic for a wide audience. I feel that the general public, or beginners of the Truth, will find it easier to understand matters of the mind. This is the first stage of our mission as a religion; first and foremost, we need to help people understand the Truth about the mind. There are various difficult topics involved in religious Truths, and many people would not be able to understand them all.

Watching various media or television programs, I find that people often assert that the mind is located in the brain; this notion may have become the accepted knowledge of today. However, medical science is misguided if it is upholding such a notion. When examining patients, many doctors probably feel as if they are operating a computer and say, "This part of the brain is the mind."

It is true that certain functions are lost when the brain is damaged, so things may seem that way. Such a view is actually based on the belief that humans are like machines, which is now becoming mainstream. From the analytical perspective, too, doctors attach electrodes to patients and see what happens when they apply an electric current to a specific area. They then conclude, "This is what happens in such and such a case."

However, this does not conform to religious Truth. If people are starting to see things in a materialistic way like this, it means that their value systems are reversed. In other words, they are viewing things upside down. This may be the case in their academic discipline as well as their actual work.

If, as a result of studying high-level academic disciplines, people come to believe that the mind is a part of the head, then there is something wrong in their academic discipline. It really is a great shame. Something is wrong if those who have endeavored to study come to believe that the mind is a part of the head, controlling and making decisions. If they regard the belief that the mind is in the chest or a little lower in the abdominal area as obsolete, then their value systems are inverted. From this, we can say that we are living in the age in which people cannot understand what resonates with their minds.

## The true nature of the "contaminated water" That runs through the academic world

The issue of the mind is a very basic and rudimentary topic, but this is where our first fight as a religion lies. If people have a firm belief that there is no such thing as the mind, then religions have almost no chance to touch their lives. It would be extremely difficult to convince or explain about the afterlife to people who openly say, "Human beings have no such thing as the mind. What are you talking about? It's just the workings of the brain, or a nerve function. We just feel something like an electrical impulse in our brain."

Many who are considered smart gradually come to hold this kind of thinking. In Buddhist terms, they would be described as having an erroneous view* or wrong view†. These people have been tainted by a view that is opposite to the righteous perspective, or the Right View. If they firmly believe that such a perspective is the orthodox style of academic studies, then they are making a terrible mistake.

In Japanese education particularly, the Ministry of Education has been integrated with the Science and Technology Agency to form the current Ministry of Education, Culture, Sports, Science and Technology, creating a risk that a scientific point of view will apply to all academic disciplines. So, there is a possibility that people will become unable to see things based on the Right View, or the Truth.

When it comes to history or religion, for example, if people do not believe anything without archaeological proof, then a figure like the first Japanese Emperor Jimmu‡ can well be perceived as nothing

---

* Erroneous views mean mistaken religious thoughts that arise from the ignorance of Buddha's Truth.

† In Buddhist terms, wrong views, or "Akuken" in Japanese, are mistaken ways of viewing things; they comprise one of the Six Worldly Delusions. One example of wrong views is an erroneous view.

‡ According to the oldest books on ancient Japanese history, *Kojiki* [Records of Ancient Matters] and *Nihon Shoki* [The Chronicles of Japan], Emperor Jimmu is said to be the very first Japanese Emperor who was enthroned in 660 BC.

more than a myth. Some even claim that Prince Shotoku* did not exist. People could claim those things, since it is not so easy to find archaeological proof. However, with regard to Prince Shotoku, there are books translated by him and records of the enemies he fought, as well as his family tree. The names of his wife and all his children are also handed down, but still some scholars claim that he is an invented character who did not exist historically.

In this sense, we can say that academic studies are becoming extensively contaminated. And the contaminated water running through academic studies will lead to deny any ideas connected with the mind and soul, or with the other world. This is something we have to break through.

I imagine that Happy Science believers are having a really tough time in their missionary work when they try to teach people about the existence of the mind. There are people who think that the mind does not exist, or that the mind can change in various ways by inputting something as if typing on a computer keyboard. These people also believe that issues regarding emotional good or evil do not exist; they just think it is the mere outcome of the operation of one's mind.

It may be true to say that when you lick salt, it tastes salty and that when you lick sugar, it tastes sweet. However, the workings of the human mind are not that simple. Even when people are all looking at the same thing, they perceive it differently depending on the person.

---

* Prince Shotoku [574 – 622 A.D.] was a Japanese statesman who acted as regent for his aunt, Empress Suiko. He is well-known for having enacted the Seventeen-Article Constitution and for having taken in Buddhism.

# 2

# The Past, Present and Future that Can Change Through the Power of the Mind

✧    ✧    ✧

## *You can change your future by changing your mind*

Humans can change various things by the power of their thoughts. It all depends on how you think about things.

Let me use human eyesight as an example. Usually, things can be seen clearly when the crystalline lens in one's eyes are adjusted and focused. This adjustment is made by the use of involuntary muscles, which cannot be moved by one's free will. For this reason, it is considered that once your eyesight worsens, it will never get better and you will have to wear contact lenses or glasses to read things clearly. It is widely believed that the refraction of light needs to be altered artificially, so that your eyes can focus on things.

In my case, however, things are different. I can alter my crystalline lens and involuntary muscles with the power of my thoughts. Whenever I find my eyesight failing, I tell myself, "OK, I must improve it to the original level. Get better, get better, get better." Then about a week later, my eyesight truly recovers. I have regenerative power, just like how a lizard can regrow its tail.

Some people can actually improve aspects of their physical body like their eyesight by strongly believing, "There is no way I cannot control my own body. I am the ruler of my body, so if I ever want to change a part of my body in a certain way, of course that is what will happen. It is just a matter of time." This would probably amaze those who are constrained by commonly accepted knowledge, but it can actually happen.

Therefore, you have to be careful. Various phenomena actually occur, not because that is how they truly are, but because you are taught to believe that is what would happen.

We humans have the power to change ourselves. We can certainly change our physical bodies. Changing our mind will lead to various other changes in life; the course of our life, relationships with others and our future will also change. For this reason, you should not simply accept others' comments about you, for example, that you are no good, or that you have no future. You must not label yourself or be convinced that you are doomed.

For example, those who label themselves as being poor and accept a poverty-stricken life can hardly make any change for the better. However, things are different for those who believe that everyone has a chance. They will think, "There must be a way to be successful at work. In the same way that baseball players become capable of hitting difficult balls by observing and studying other successful hitters, I could also find some secrets to success if I closely observe people who are good at making money. So, I will observe rich people around me and study any differences between them and myself. And once I find the differences, I'll imitate the good ones."

It is essential to think this way. If you imitate someone for five or ten years, without realizing it you could become like him or her. This can actually happen. You can change your life in this way.

### Konosuke Matsushita changed his life Into a golden one, including his past

Previously, I have repeatedly taught, "Basically, you cannot change the past. You cannot change the historical fact that something was done, but you can change the future." It is certainly true that you can change the future while you cannot change the past; this accords with general opinion. In terms of religious truth, however, you can take it one step further; the past can also be changed. We can change the past.

My second son Masaki Okawa* gave a lecture on his book, *Okawa Ryuho Meigen-shu Sozo-teki ni Naritai Anata e 123 no Kingen* [literally, "The Collected Wisdom of Ryuho Okawa 123 Golden Truths for Those of You Who Want to Be Creative," Masaki Okawa, (Tokyo: IRH Press, 2015)] at Yokohama Shoshinkan, and in that lecture he said as follows: "Successful people all experienced hardships and failures when they were young. However, when they have achieved great success, they say that their success was thanks to what must surely have been their wretched past. This is their common

---

* Masaki Okawa has assumed a managerial position at Happy Science, giving lectures to the public and publishing books on various themes.

trait. It may seem strange, but all highly successful people make such remarks."

There is a reason for this. Actually, people cannot see their past differently with just a minor success or a small promotion at work, but when they enter the path to great success that fundamentally transforms their life, their entire past becomes completely beautified.

Take, for example, the life of Konosuke Matsushita,* the founder of Panasonic. As a boy, he suffered great hardships; his father had failed in speculating in the rice market, so Konosuke had to quit elementary school and was sent to Osaka to work as an apprentice. Instead of going to school, he worked very hard in all sorts of miscellaneous work. But he gradually learned to form his own company and actually started the business with two other people. His company eventually grew large enough to employ as many as tens of thousands of people, with factories around the world.

Upon achieving that level of success, Konosuke would say that he owed his success to the lack of his academic achievement. The average person, or someone who had only achieved some minor success, could never say anything like that. For example, someone who dropped out of elementary school but later was able to earn as much as a university graduate would not be able to say that. With that level of success, it would be hard to say that having dropped out of elementary school made him or her successful.

---

* Konosuke Matsushita [1894 – 1989] was a well-known Japanese industrialist who started his own business in 1918 and developed it to eventually become the present-day Panasonic, one of the largest Japanese multinational electronics companies. He is often referred to as a "god of management" in Japan for his business philosophy.

However, Konosuke was different. Despite having had to drop out of elementary school, he attained a position to employ people who had completed university or graduate school, manage these subordinates to make various products, and then give them praise or pay them bonuses. He became renowned in the world, and was even featured on the cover of *Time* magazine.

The comments of Konosuke Matsushita include, "I became successful because I dropped out of elementary school and had no educational background," "Since I didn't study and had no knowledge, I asked others about things I didn't know and tried to employ people cleverer than I was. So, I employed a lot of clever people and tried to bring out their talents. This is how I became successful," "I was of poor health and often had to miss work. So, I created a department system, where every business unit of the company operates independently, and entrusted people with the work, so that the business could run even when I was ill. This resulted in nurturing many talented managers and thus developing our company." This shows how success not only improves the present, but also goes back into the past and changes everything into gold.

## *Walt Disney achieved great success*
## *With a cartoon mouse*

Whether one can change the past into gold depends on the level of success. Another example of someone who achieved great success was Walt Disney. His tremendous success made him a worldwide figure; there is probably no one who hasn't heard of him. Some people in countries or regions where electrical access is limited may not know him, but most people in places with wide electrical usage most likely know about Disney.

According to the Disney legend, when he was young, he was poor and lived in a run-down apartment, where a mouse would run in and out of holes in the wall. But he observed the mouse closely and started to wonder what would happen if he made it into a cartoon character. That is how he came up with the idea of Mickey Mouse and became fabulously rich.

An average person could have probably come up with a character like a costumed PR mascot of today. It might be possible to make some money by marketing a mouse mascot as a stand-alone business. You could be the first to create and sell cartoon mouse products to the world, which would allow you to profit and make your life easier. However, that level of success is not enough to turn your entire life into gold. It is only possible with a level of success where your business expands, enabling you to build theme parks like Disneyland, attracting tens of millions of people every year, and to grow a lot of other related businesses throughout the world. When this happens, you will come to see that having lived in a run-down apartment with a mouse as your friend was the very source of all your success.

Generally speaking, things would not turn out like that if an ordinary person lived in a room with mice running around in it. For example, someone may continue studying for years trying to pass the bar examination after graduating and even turning 30. That person would definitely complain that because of the mouse problem, he could not concentrate and failed the exam year after year. He would thus attribute his failure to the mouse. In this way, the same conditions can produce different results.

When you have achieved great success far surpassing common circumstances, all your experiences will turn into light, including those in your long-gone past. Even someone who lost family members in the Hiroshima atomic bombing, for example, would be able to say upon achieving great success that his or her very experience had inspired him or her to work very hard; everything would be transformed into gold. Or someone who had lost family members in a terrible natural disaster would be able to consider that experience to be the reason for his or her current success.

In this sense, the past, present and future can actually change. Humans can change everything with the power of the mind or the power of thought.

# 3

# My Messages for Modern People Who Do Not Know How to Control their Minds

✧　　✧　　✧

## *Not recognizing the mind is like Riding in a car with no steering wheel*

The mind is an actual entity, and your state of mind will change your life and open your future. Those who have awakened to this truth are like people who have learned how to steer a car and can drive freely down the road. Conversely, those who believe that the mind does not exist are like people who are riding in a car without knowing there is a steering wheel.

It would be horrific to ride in a car with just the gas and brake and without the steering wheel. The car will move forward when you step on the gas pedal, but it will most likely bump into something unless you step on the brake and stop. You can only move forward or stop, so you basically cannot drive on anything but a straight road. But it must be terrifying to continue driving forward in a car with only the gas and brake when you have other cars running in front of and behind you. I would not want to drive such a car. After all, not only do you need the gas and brake, but also a steering wheel to drive.

In reality, however, there are people who believe that there is no steering wheel, or who do not realize that they are the ones who can do the steering. These people do not understand that their own thoughts have brought about their current situation. They do not understand when others say, "Your car will turn right when you turn the steering wheel right, and left when you turn it left. It goes straight forward when you keep the wheel straight. To keep moving on the straight path is the state of the Middle Way. If you suddenly steer to the right or the left, you can easily crash into something. You can easily die this way, if you choose to."

In fact, people can die easily, if they want to. For example, eating only hamburgers or steak all the time would most probably ruin your health and you would end up dying young. I do not intend to discredit any restaurant, but I imagine even workers at such a restaurant could not eat such food every day. If someone working at a place serving beef dishes eats beef at every meal, he or she would certainly find it unbearable; that person is bound to develop some kind of illness. That is how things go.

To use a metaphor, our physical body is like a car, which has a steering wheel, gas and brake. That is the basic structure; and additionally of course, it has a fuel tank and other functions such as air-conditioning. The one driving the car is the soul and the car body itself is our physical body. The truth is that the soul dwells in the physical body, and this is analogous to a person driving a car. Furthermore, in the human soul there is a part called the "mind" which thinks and makes decisions. This is the essential view of life.

## *The reason why I continuously give Many spiritual messages and teachings*

People without the above view of life may perhaps think of themselves as an automatic car installed with artificial intelligence, driving on its own. Or some may think they are being operated by remote control. Yet others may think of themselves as being the mechanical part of a car that runs to its destination based on the input data. There are many people like this. However, these are the mistakes that have arisen due to modern-day education.

You need to change such ways of thinking to achieve true happiness. Of course, you can choose either way of thinking, but since you have the right to decide for yourself whether to be happy or unhappy, it is better to choose the option that truly benefits you.

Some people may say that it is ridiculous to believe in the other world because no one has ever come back from there. But that is simply not true. Every year I introduce many messages and thoughts from the spirits in the other world. I also make them available for view in video format. I am not a comic dialogist who can act and perform for such long hours. I have graduated from the University of Tokyo, Faculty of Law, and there is no reason for me to behave in a way that would group me with the likes of con men and swindlers. I have the ability to pass national exams of Japan without difficulty and I believe I am qualified and talented enough to be successful should I choose any path of life.

I am such a person who chose to leave his job for what he believed to be important, and is now giving teachings. There is absolutely no reason why I should need to deceive people. The reason I chose to abandon my secular career to teach the Truth was because I was urged to save the many people who were suffering from going down the wrong path. That is why I now teach and publish many books on the Truth.

## Happy Science has been keeping All of my teachings as records

Some people are quick to be skeptical, but I entered this path of religion not of my own volition but because I received a calling. Newly established religious groups probably include many people who commit frauds and scams but such groups tend to remain small and do not become large. Some of them may come in a guise of having an intellectual framework, but their fraudulent elements will come to light in the long run through their loss of reputation and credibility.

My lectures are not only published as books, but also made public through CDs and DVDs. Everything has been recorded; nothing is concealed. Only slight alterations such as edits of prepositions are made when they are transcribed into book form, but basically everything is left the way it was said. We have everything from our first session [the lecture given on November 23, 1986, entitled, "Regarding the Launching of Happy Science"] to the present day, so there is absolutely no trickery. There is proof. Unlike other organizations, I do not have other people write for me. I write about my own experiences and ideas.

The common starting pattern of religious groups five to six hundred years ago in Japan was for someone like a female farmer to hear the voice of some spirit and tell people about what she heard. In my case, however, I have the foundation of a first rate education in academic subjects of this world. I express teachings only after I have judged them to be true through my filter of reason and intelligence. Happy Science books have been reputed to be highly intelligent, logical and rational. This trait has attracted many people with scientific backgrounds, as well as many with social intelligence. There are also many CEOs and managers who use my writings as textbooks, not only because my teachings cover management but also the laws of the mind. They find my teachings about the fundamental study of human beings beneficial.

### Knowing the truth about everlasting life Is essential

When you meet someone who denies the existence of the mind or soul, please be persistent and tell him or her, "You are free to think the way you do, but in your way of thinking you regard yourself as a part of a machine, which is a very self-deprecating image. Are you truly satisfied with such a view of life that a human being is a kind of machine with the mind somewhere in the body serving to operate it?"

Many people today believe in the theory of happiness that is confined only to this world and think, "Everything ends with death. So, when I die, I don't mind my body being cremated and the ashes being thrown away in a field or scattered at sea. Just do whatever suits you." But the reason I teach about the existence of the mind and soul is because the essence of a human being is everlasting, that humans have eternal life.

The truth is that humans live eternally through the past and the future, that everyone has a past before birth and a future after death. It is essential to lead one's life on earth based on this knowledge, as those who do not know this will have a hard time after death. This knowledge is extremely important because it will lead people to live a life of great value.

There are people who cannot think about the existence of the mind and soul. These people believe that life is only limited to this world and everything ends with death. So, they may think that all they have to do to prepare for death is to sort out their end-of-life affairs such as securing a will for family left behind. However, death is not the end. It is the start of a new beginning, because we are living an everlasting life.

## *How to spend each precious day of life, Which lasts about 30,000 days*

The time we have in this life is generally between twenty and thirty thousand days. That is all we have. You may think you have plenty of time, but actually you don't have that much. Living for thirty thousand days means you will be over 80 years old.

I have already spent around twenty thousand days. I wonder

how many days I have left, since the average life is twenty-odd thousand days. Thinking about how many more days we have left will make us keenly aware of each day that slips by. We can barely live past thirty thousand. Each day slips by. So, what we do in a day is extremely important. It is very important not to waste a single day.

Those who are close to my age should have already spent more than twenty thousand days in this life. Some of you may be younger and some may be older, but we need to remind ourselves that it is not so easy to live over thirty thousand days. This being so, every single day is very precious. We have to treasure each day, and how we spend each day is extremely important. Philosophy and Zen Buddhism are ultimately advocating a similar idea.

# 4

# Live Every Day Transforming Yourself

✧ ✧ ✧

## *The story of the wild ducks that lost the ability to fly*

More than a century ago the Danish philosopher Soren Kierkegaard[*] introduced the following story: In the countryside of Denmark, an elderly man kindly fed the wild ducks that would fly there every year.

---

[*] Soren Kierkegaard [1813 – 1855] was a philosopher and thinker born in Denmark, who had great influence on today's existential philosophy and dialectical theology. His writings include *The Sickness Unto Death*, *Either/Or*, and *The Concept of Anxiety*.

As they kept feeding there, some of them lost their habit of flying south when the weather turned cold. They got fatter and fatter and ended up losing the ability to fly.

One day, however, the kind old man suddenly died. The wild ducks were in trouble, because they had become so fat that they could no longer fly. Having already lost their habit of migration, they did not know what to do. In the end, when the spring thaw flooded in, they all drowned.

## *The existentialist philosopher Soren Kierkegaard who Told the story of the wild ducks*

Kierkegaard is said to be the founder of existential philosophy. He was almost unknown when he lived, but was later made famous by the German philosopher Martin Heidegger.*

Kierkegaard was born to a woman who formerly worked as a housemaid. Having suffered from illness, he had a rather unhappy early life. In his final years, he published pamphlets entitled *The Moment* and was critical of churches. He would comment in the following way: "You are far from being saved. You are mistaken if you believe you can go to a good place after death by praying and purifying your mind in church only on Sunday, when in fact you are

---

*Martin Heidegger [1889 – 1976] was a German philosopher who is said to be one of the greatest thinkers of the 20th century. He was a teacher of the political theorist Hannah Arendt. When the Nazi regime was established in 1933, he assumed the position of the Rector of the University of Freiburg but resigned one year later. His works include *Being and Time*.

living in a spiritually neglectful way from Monday to Saturday. Every single day is important for humans. Making no efforts from Monday to Saturday and praying only on Sunday will hardly save you."

Immersed in teaching such a philosophy, one day he collapsed on the street and met a miserable end. This was the kind of man who was at the start of existentialist philosophy. His story of the above-mentioned wild ducks is one of his well-known teachings.

## *The IBM spirit: do not become a tamed wild duck*

Thomas Watson Jr., who headed and enlarged the IBM company following his father, later used the story of the wild duck to teach the IBM spirit; he taught the importance of staying wild, without becoming like a tamed duck which had lost the ability to fly after being fed by others.

He would tell his employees, "Do not be content with just maintaining the status quo. We never know when danger will strike, or when we will go under. So, always be on alert for danger. Every day must be a serious battle, and every day we must innovate. We need such a hunger, a sense of crisis, day after day. There will be no future unless we live life giving everything we've got." This attitude made IBM into a global company.

## *Every day, make efforts, transform yourself, take on Challenges and cope with changes in your environment*

Watson's way of thinking is also very important for all of us. You might be thinking that things are fine because you are making a living, but you never know when your life will change due to some external circumstance, for example, the emergence of a rival business. Even large corporations are going bankrupt now, one after another. Many leading manufacturers are also on the brink of bankruptcy, and some have even gone under. Overseas rivals may emerge, or you may lose out to domestic rivals.

Companies such as Uniqlo [Fast Retailing Co., Ltd. of Japan] seems to be conquering the world markets, but even they would go under if the exchange rate changes. When the yen was strong, they were able to open numerous stores overseas with lower expenditures, but if the exchange rate falls, meaning more yen to the dollar, they would surely go bankrupt. Companies like Toyota that profit from exports may report a gain of around 10 billion yen [approx. 100 million dollars] with a one-yen drop in the exchange rate, but conversely, discount stores which depend on imports will start closing down. Those companies that took advantage of the strong yen and moved production overseas would most likely be crippled if the yen weakens, so their future is uncertain.

Therefore, we must always bear in mind the spirit of the wild duck. We never know what will happen, and this is a very scary point. In our lives, too, we must live every day with a sense of danger. We must have the kind of "DNA" that urges us to make efforts, transform ourselves, take on new challenges, and weather the changes in our environment every day. Without such DNA, we can hardly survive, be it an individual or an organization.

## *The world of religion, which was thought to be Everlasting, is facing the danger of extinction*

Religions were thought to be everlasting, but when I take a look at the number of religious groups, many seem to be on the verge of disappearing. Happy Science transmits my lectures throughout Japan and the world. Some religious groups in and near the areas covered by our broadcasts may be fearful that they might someday be pushed out by the presence of Happy Science; some groups may already have disappeared.

In the 1980s, around the time when Happy Science was established, many new religious groups emerged in Japan. New ones appeared one after another in the 1970s and 1980s, and we had many rivals at the time. In these 30 years, however, many of them have lost popularity and disappeared. Although society has not given any clear evaluation on religions, some groups persevered and grew while others disappeared. This is a harsh outcome, but the principle of the survival of the fittest also applies to the world of religion.

Traditional religions seem to be aware that unless they make efforts now, they can hardly survive. For example, Higashi Hongan-ji Temple [a school of True Pure Land Buddhism] in Asakusa, Tokyo, invited well-known scholar and critic Shoichi Watanabe to give a lecture for the commemoration of the 70th anniversary of the end of WWII, and opened it to the public for free. The teachings of their founder Shinran, which just encourage people to seek salvation by praying to Amitabha Buddha, do not explain, for example, how to evaluate the 70 years after WWII. They cannot comment on various world affairs, unlike Happy Science that gives its own opinions. That is why they invited a critic to give a lecture with free admission in order to attract people.

## *Reconsider the safety myth, in which people believe Everything has been all right so far*

The aforementioned story of the wild ducks that lost the ability to fly by being fed by an old man can also be used as a metaphor to talk about the danger of the national regime. Japan, for example, can be compared to the wild duck that receives nourishing food from the kind old man, America. As it eats the food, Japan is assured that it no longer needs to fly south and can safely survive winter.

However, if birds lose their ability to fly, they could die from drowning should the water from the melted snow come flooding down. In the same manner, if Japan believes it is safe as long as it adheres to the safety myth, one day it may suddenly come to an unfortunate end; there may come a time when the "kind old man" no longer provides Japan with "food."\* So, Japan needs to think about what to do in case that occurs.

I cited this example because various disputes are now going on in the Japanese Diet concerning national defense. Ordinary birds would fly south to find food in winter, but the Japanese people tend to think, "We are not the same as ordinary birds. We have someone to feed us so we do not need to fly south." However, they need to be aware that they may not always be safe and sound.

Here, I do not intend to go into a deeper discussion concerning the Constitution of Japan, but I just want to alert Japanese people who feel assured because of the safety myth. Japan needs to basically go back to the starting point, and think deeply about how a nation should be and how other countries are securing themselves. Not doing this and just feeling safe with the ongoing conventional way could someday jeopardize Japan.

The same applies to countries, as well as individuals, companies and any small businesses. Your business may suddenly go under with an appearance of a rival when you thought you were doing well. The mere opening of a rival shop across the street or next door may cause your business to go bankrupt. So, you always need to be on the alert.

---

\*The Japanese postwar constitution states in Article 9 that Japan renounces any capability of war, so Japan signed a treaty in 1951 to strengthen its ties with the U.S. in military cooperation. In the current Japan–U.S. Security Treaty, the U.S. agrees to help defend Japan against any foreign adversaries.

# 5

# Think About How to Make The Best Use of Your Mind and Live Life to the Fullest

✧   ✧   ✧

## *The experiences your soul gained in life will be carried Over after death*

People who have skillfully lived their twenty or thirty thousand days of life, who have lived with wisdom, can have a good future in the afterlife. To have an afterlife means that even after a person dies, his or her soul lives on. Some religions teach that after death, people's souls will be absorbed into something like an ocean and remain underwater as tiny particles, but such a view of afterlife is not true.

The truth is that the human soul has individual character that is carried over to the other world. People have a gender in this life, male or female, and when their souls leave this world for the other, they retain their consciousness, name, gender, and character gained through their knowledge and experiences in this life. They recognize themselves as such until the next time they are born. In this way, your life experience as an individual basically continues in the other world as well. That is why the way one lives in this world is extremely important.

## *Use your time in life wisely and live life to the fullest*

Life consists of only twenty or thirty thousand days, so it is best to make good use of your time and live life to the fullest. Instead of blaming others, change what you can change for yourself, and overcome any difficulties skillfully using your own steering wheel, gas and brake.

Not only can you change your future, but you can also change your past. Some countries keep attributing their current unhappiness to past misery, but the very act of doing so is already making them unhappy. As long as they keep blaming others, they can never be happy.

If a country is truly shining now, it should be able to forgive the past and no longer speak of it. But if that country keeps saying that there is unhappiness today because of what happened 70 or 80 years ago, it means that their current government is not doing a good job. Surely, that is the case. Since the current government is so ineffective, the politicians blame the past or other countries to divert the people's attention. Those who cannot understand this, unfortunately, can hardly be called the leading intellectuals of today.

In this chapter, I have focused on the topic of the mind and my main message was that we all have a mind of which we have total control. We can make use of it with our own free will 100 percent, so it is important to live skillfully by using it. Happy Science gives many teachings about how to make the best use of your mind and live life to the fullest. The 2015 bestseller *The Laws of Wisdom* (Tokyo: HS

Press, 2015) in particular, teaches how to refine your wisdom and bring out its value like a diamond. No other religions teach this. It would make me happy if you could understand this difference and learn the Truth deeply.

Chapter TWO

# How to Become an Attractive Person

*The Power to Turn Critics into Fans*

# *1*

# How to Bring Out One's Attractiveness Is a Deep Topic to Consider

This chapter describes the essential points to become an attractive person. If you master this content, you should be able to succeed in almost everything. In this regard, this topic is rather deep.

This is the transcription of the lecture I gave at Tokyo Shoshinkan, one of the Happy Science religious facilities. On that day, the monitor at the venue showed that the event was mostly attended by our older members. On seeing it I thought to myself, "This audience might make it harder for me to give a lecture on this topic because it is generally very tough for older people to bring out their attractiveness from this point on compared to younger ones. This is going to be harder work than I expected today."

Young people, for example, still have much room to develop themselves to be more attractive. But as we grow older, it becomes more difficult to evolve, and this of course goes for me as well as for you. The question is, "How can you bring out your attractiveness in this condition that is more difficult?" I hope the content of this lecture has some positive effect, however slightly, on each and every one of you.

Incidentally, the day after I gave this lecture, the well-known Japanese scholar and critic Shoichi Watanabe* also spoke at Tokyo Shoshinkan. One can learn how to be attractive by observing how he talks to others. In his conversations, Mr. Watanabe always praises the person to whom he is speaking. He always lowers himself by mentioning his inferiority complex or some mistake he made. He opens up and reveals slight chinks in his armor, and praises the person he is talking to. Also, he always ends the conversation in a way that leaves people feeling good. This is how Mr. Watanabe usually talks to others. He seems to understand very well how to make himself appealing.

---

*Shoichi Watanabe [1930 – 2017] was an English scholar and emeritus professor at Sophia University in Japan. He was also one of the foremost Japanese critics, writing books and giving lectures as an influential conservative opinion-leader.

# 2

# Points to Consider When Praising Someone

✧   ✧   ✧

## *Praise will invite a negative reaction*
## *Unless you speak the truth*

When I try to praise people in the same way as Mr. Watanabe does, it does not always work out for me. That is because I am a man of religion; I must speak the truth. When I was younger, I often read in various books that things would generally go well by praising people because they would have a good impression of you, and there was a time when I intentionally tried to praise others.

However, as I became a religious leader and our organization grew larger, things started to change. The number of people I needed to guide increased, and when I praised them in a slightly exaggerated or flattering way, it often had a negative effect. Some of the people I praised took my words to be unequivocally and unchangeably true. Then later, when others evaluated them lowly or my assessment of them lowered, they reacted and started to give blame instead. As such experiences increased, I came to feel that it had become harder for me to praise people.

Looking back over the more than 30 years of Happy Science history, there have been all kinds of people but, comparatively speaking, people I have scolded have tended to stay in executive positions for longer than those I have praised. People that I have scolded on multiple occasions, in particular, are mostly still with us.

On the other hand, people who were only praised and never scolded tended to leave us. Whether they had made a mistake at work or could no longer cope with their job, when these people were demoted from their former positions for whatever reason, they often had dissatisfaction. This caused others to think of them poorly and triggered criticism, and they ended up leaving the organization. There was even a person who accused us saying, "I cannot accept this demotion because I was someone who Master Okawa praised." This shows how difficult it is to praise others.

## *Do not try to please everyone; Praise others only as much as you can handle*

Some books say that praising others will make you popular, allowing you to influence them. In reality, however, things do not often go that way. Why is that? It is probably because the writers' ideas spring from a sales-like approach, that is to say, to boost one's sales performance through a one-on-one negotiation with a customer. They assume that you can increase the number of your loyal customers and become successful by pleasing others. That is why they advise you to smile a lot and make others feel good by praising them, thereby giving a good impression of yourself. This is the general motif that underlies their idea. However, this approach does not align with my position as a religious leader.

This topic, "how to become an attractive person," naturally includes concerns of men and women, about how to attract someone of the opposite sex. But in my case, through the psychic power of divine hearing,* every night I can hear the voices of both male and female believers saying, "I love you, Master Okawa." Although I am grateful for their love, I am not sure how to respond to them, so this can be a really difficult situation.

You may well appear to be attractive if you go around trying to please everyone. However, you could be held responsible for other people's responses or reactions, so it is worthy to note that your praise must be within your capability to bear responsibility. It is important to refrain from praising someone more than you can handle.

---

* Divine hearing is one of the Six Divine Supernatural Powers, which allows one to hear the voice of the spirits in the other world. Refer to *The Laws of the Sun* (New York: IRH Press, 2013).

# 3

# People Observe Others in Public and in Private

✦    ✦    ✦

### *Are you behaving differently when no one Is watching?*

"How to Become an Attractive Person" was a title suggested to me by those in management at Happy Science. They probably expected to hear some tips about how to move forward with our missionary work as a religion, as well as how to get the support and votes from many people for our political party, the Happiness Realization Party. I felt their wish to receive some explicit advice to promote these two activities.

Giving advice on such matters is actually quite challenging because sometimes situations within the group and outside are different. Sometimes things do not go as we wish, or can even produce the opposite outcome. For example, someone considered attractive inside the Happy Science group can be seen as not so attractive outside, or someone considered unattractive inside can be seen as attractive outside. Both cases can happen, so this is a difficult theme to talk about.

On April 7, 2013, I went to the Happy Science Academy Kansai School to give a lecture during its first entrance ceremony [the lecture title was *Kofuku-no-Kagaku Gakuen no Mirai ni Kitai-suru* (literally, "My Expectations for the Future of Happy Science Academy")]. On my way back on the bullet train, I happened to spot a man who has had a long career as a singer and actor; he attracts tens of thousands of people to his concerts and appears in detective dramas, too. He sat in the seat just in front of me, facing some other people—maybe his musician friends or staff members. They were conversing loudly among themselves.

Then suddenly, he lowered the back of his seat, which stopped right before it hit my face. I thought he should have at least said a word of apology. He certainly did not make a good impression on me to have suddenly lowered the back of his seat without any notice. Every time he went to the toilet in the bullet train he was accompanied by a bodyguard, so people on the train easily recognized him. But he seemed to believe he was well disguised by his sunglasses.

When he got off the bullet train at Shinagawa Station, his eyes focused on me through the window; it seemed that someone pointed me out to him. I was sitting in the seat behind him, so he probably did not notice me, but when he realized who I was, he stared at me for a while. But it was a little too late; he had shown a rather rude side of his character. In this way, some people, although they are wildly popular in concerts or other events, actually behave differently in their private life, when they think they are not being watched.

## *Politicians and candidates are being observed in both Their public and private lives*

I have written in my books about similar cases involving politicians. For example, I once saw a Japanese foreign minister snoring in front of me as soon as he got on the plane, or another Cabinet minister drinking heavily in first class on a plane [refer to books such as *Kyoiku no Shimei* (literally, "The Mission of Education") (Tokyo: IRH Press, 2013) and *Bi no Dendo-shi no Shimei* (literally, "The Mission of a Missionary of Beauty") (Tokyo: IRH Press, 2015)].

You never know when or where someone is watching you. Politicians, in particular, need to be aware that they are being watched in both their public and private lives; they can never know where they will win or lose someone's vote. The same is true with those who plan to stand as candidates in the future; they also need to be aware that every aspect of their behavior is being observed.

Some people say the right things but act differently, but this attitude is not good. Politicians may use various techniques to gain popularity, but ultimately their true character will show through. If their popularity is only superficial, the adoration will eventually pass and disappear. They need to be aware of this.

## *A change in status will alter people's assessment*

Around the time I started Happy Science, Honorable Adviser Saburo Yoshikawa,* my own father, would say to me, "You are not good-looking," "Your voice is no good," and "You don't look as good as an actor." He made harsh remarks on various traits of mine, and his judgments were indeed to the point.

But when I gave my first lecture on March 8, 1987, entitled, "The Principles of Happiness," I was amazed to have had both positive and negative reactions to my voice. Probably those who liked to hear Japanese ballads tended to like my voice, whereas those who disliked them did not. Everyone has different tastes, and it is difficult to appeal to everyone.

It is no easy matter to please a variety of people with different personalities or tastes, or to attract them. For example, you may expect that someone academically strong can gain the respect of others and be popular. However, this is not always the case. There are so many examples where this is not the case, so you cannot make sweeping generalizations.

Being good at studies does not always lead you to acquire intellectual virtue and make you popular, because while studying increases your knowledge, your views on others can be harsher and you can end up being judgmental. Knowing a lot of things can make you notice others' bad points and lead you to view people rather

---

*Honorable Adviser Saburo Yoshikawa [1921 – 2003] helped Ryuho Okawa from the very start of Happy Science, by serving as a questioner and helping to publish books of spiritual messages. He also published his own books and gave lectures on the Truth.

judgmentally. This trait can make you less appealing.

In fact, I, myself, often point out what people need to improve, but my situation has changed from when I was young; people receive my words slightly differently now. I can now boldly declare that I am the National Teacher and can sternly scold people, including those who have high social standing. But when I was young, I was bitterly reprimanded for speaking impudently. I have always said exactly what is on my mind, but my change in status-altered people's assessment of me.

# 4

# Looking Back at My Own Experience

This chapter deals with how to become an attractive person, but it is much easier to think of ways to become less appealing. I have plenty of real-life examples on getting yourself disliked by others, how to get scolded, or how to be labeled useless. It may be that the Japanese people do not usually praise others much, but I can recall lots of cases when my behavior triggered anger in others. I have plenty of experiences to reflect upon.

## *Case 1: At a welcome party for new employees*

When I had just began working at a trading company, the section I was assigned to kindly held a welcome party. All the colleagues in the section were going to gather in a private room at a restaurant to welcome me to the team, and I was very delighted. I thought I was certainly the guest of honor since it was a party to welcome the new recruit, so when I walked into the room, I took my seat at the very back of the room.

However, the senior colleagues who arrived after me all glared at me. I had no idea why everyone had such an unpleasant expression. I could not understand what was wrong with me sitting at the back of the room when I was the guest of honor. But this incident was the beginning of my being scolded often by senior colleagues.

One of my senior colleagues explained, "Listen. New employees are meant to sit by the door." When I responded, "But it's hard to relax sitting near the door because of people coming in and out of the room," he angrily said, "And that is why new employees should sit there." I finally understood what I had done. I had simply sat down where I could relax since I didn't want to be bothered by people carrying food and drinks in and out of the room. So, I ended up getting a good scolding. In a spiritual sense, of course, I should essentially have been held in high regard, but my colleagues at that time did not know that.

## Case 2: *The Mito-Komon incident*

About three to six months after I joined the company, I heard widespread gossip about myself being called "that guy." I wondered what they meant by that. They would say, "You are the Mito-Komon incident guy!" I was still not quite sure what it was that I had done, and later found out the following story that was widely spread among my colleagues.

My university graduation ceremony was held around the end of March, and on the same day I also had to attend the company's entrance ceremony for new recruits. The company's headquarters was in Osaka, so the entrance ceremony was held there, and the new recruits were to meet there for a luncheon party. I had taken part in the university's graduation ceremony from nine to ten that morning and then, having no time to go home, got on the bullet train to head straight for Osaka from Tokyo.

On the bullet train, there happened to be a few fellow new recruits of the same company and I was talking with them on the way to Osaka. In the conversation, I was asked which university I had graduated from, so I responded by holding up my diploma cylinder. It had "The University of Tokyo, Faculty of Law" written in gold letters on a black brocaded background. I never thought this would be made into an issue, but it was spread as "the Mito-Komon incident [*laughs*]."

In Japan, Mito-Komon was a popular period drama on TV inspired by the former vice-shogun Mitsukuni Tokugawa. He would disguise himself as a merchant while investigating crimes and the climax of the show was when he revealed his identity to the criminals by holding up the official seal with his family crest, saying, "Behold!" Apparently, the way I held up my diploma reminded my colleagues of that drama, and I was made fun of on various occasions for the next six months.

I simply thought it would be boastful for me to say that I had graduated from the University of Tokyo, especially in public, so I simply showed them the diploma cylinder without saying anything. But the story snowballed into one where I had purposely brandished the case. I thought people would dislike me for bragging if I actually said the name of my university, so I was shocked to learn of their reaction to what I did. There seems to have been a big gap between Japanese common sense and what I considered to be common sense.

## Case 3: In a taxi shared with senior workers

A similar event happened when I shared a taxi with the senior colleagues in my section. When a few of us caught a taxi, I thought it would be impolite to expect my senior colleagues to open the door and have them slide across the back seat to the other side. So, I got in first and sat behind the driver. I felt I should let them sit next to the door, so they could get in and out easily, or sit in the passenger seat where there was a better view.

However, I was later told by one of those senior colleagues, "You probably don't know this, but where you sat was where the most senior person sits." I remember that he then taught me the order of ranking for the taxi seats. It seemed that I always ended up thinking the opposite of what ordinary people thought. I sat behind the driver because I wanted my seniors to avoid the trouble of going all the way in, but I was actually scolded for it.

## Case 4: Hailing a taxi late at night in America

Another blunder was when I was working in America. We worked late one evening and tried to hail a taxi, but we could not get one to stop. Robberies increase late at night in New York, so getting a taxi to stop is not easy; raising your hand works at daytime, but that will not always do at night.

Then, three female American colleagues started hailing a taxi by hitching up their skirts like a cancan performance. I burst out laughing because it reminded me of a scene from a dance revue. Then, one of my senior colleagues got angry with me and said, "You just don't have a clue, do you? It's really hard to get a cab to stop at this time of night, so they are doing their very best to get one for us by using their sex appeal—raising their skirts a bit and showing their legs to attract the drivers' attention. You should be ashamed of yourself for laughing."

I have given you a few examples here, but I could give you many more. It was a really terrible time for me. In this regard, I can certainly teach you in many ways how to get yourself disliked by others, but it is truly hard to teach how to become an attractive person.

## Case 5: Walking around with lots of books in my bag

People praise you for studying when you are a student, but once you are a working adult, studying in the presence of others does not earn you any praise. For example, I always used to carry lots of books around with me, and I was told things like, "You never change, do you? Are you going to be like this your whole life?" When I replied, "Yes. I carry a lot of books around, so I can get one out of my bag whenever I have time to read on the train," they would say, "Ah. So, you intend to keep that up your whole life?"

We never seemed to be on the same wavelength. I had no idea at the time that I should have kept my colleagues from seeing how hard I was studying. In this way, I was completely out of step with what society sees as common sense.

## Clothing: An example of how value judgments change When circumstances change

Strangely enough, things changed completely when I became involved in religion. Other people started to listen to and respect my opinions. This was really surprising, and I actually wished I had someone to explain to me what was going on.

For example, on the day I was to give this lecture, it was

suggested that I wear pinkish orange clothes. I could not but double-check with my assistants if the choice was really all right. If I were still working for a company and were to wear such colors to work, it would cause quite a stir. If, after coming back from vacation for example, I suddenly showed up looking like that, my colleagues would wonder if I had gone off the rails.

What is more, the tie suggested for me to wear with those clothes was rainbow-colored. When I asked my assistants, "Are you really sure this is OK for today's lecture?" I was told, "Yes, these colors really suit you." I remember feeling a little odd when I wore those clothes. Apparently, there is no denying that society's value judgments change in various ways with the change in one's circumstances.

# 5

# Essential Points to Become an Attractive Person

✧     ✧    ✧

## *One attribute of a leader is the ability to Recover quickly from a setback*

I have talked about several personal episodes; these experiences made me feel that I had better accept being on the receiving end of criticism. Those who quickly change themselves in response to the criticism of others are the type of people who just follow social standards. In other words, they may be average people who can follow instructions and orders and be easily used by others. On the other hand, those who recover immediately even after being criticized are unchangeable. This ability to bounce back to one's original state is an important quality.

Apparently, those who have the ability to bounce back quickly from situations that would usually make people feel low, gradually develop a kind of divine power. In a sense, this is one of the attributes of a leader. It is essential for a leader to somehow get back up on his or her feet and keep moving forward after an event that would leave average people feeling disappointed, sad or despondent. It is very hard for average people to do this; they will usually fall into a prolonged period of self-pity.

When I was young, there were many times when, at the end of the day, I would think, "It really was an embarrassing day. I wish I could crawl under a rock. Is my life going to keep on like this?" Numerous times I experienced such thoughts of self-pity and self-loathing welling up from inside, though this is of course nothing to boast about.

I now recommend people to practice self-reflection, but in the past I was in no position to tell other people to do so. So many times I would feel self-hatred, thinking, "I wish I could just crawl into a hole and hide," "I really embarrassed myself today," or "I didn't realize this particular kind of common sense." But now, I have a good habit of checking to see if I made progress in some area or if I made good use of the day before going to sleep.

I am ashamed to say that, when I was young, my state of mind was not so different from that of Osamu Dazai [1909 - 1948], the Japanese novelist who committed suicide. He would say that being alive was a source of embarrassment, and I, too, would strongly feel that way. Later, however, I changed my attitude; I would recover before too long whenever something happened to make me feel down. I gradually realized how surprisingly important it was to have the ability to recover within a few days or by the following week.

## *People who are full of self-pity appear self-centered*

In the final count, other people are not really concerned about your self-pity. While they may sympathize with you a bit initially, they will not want to be around you after a while. I'm sure this is what would happen. People will not keep listening to someone who goes on and on about something he or she cannot get over.

Those who pity themselves are not aware that they are actually taking love from others. They just see themselves as a kind of tragic Cinderella who deserves to be pitied. But basically, people who always desperately need to comfort themselves do not think of others. Thus, they appear to be very self-centered. The problem is that they are not aware of their self-centered appearance. All they care about is some event in the past, where they were hurt or criticized by others. They need to change this attitude as soon as they can, and they can overcome this tendency with their thoughts.

## *When there is a nail of failure, hammer it out*
## *With a new nail of positive thoughts*

In one of the early Happy Science collections of spiritual messages, you can find the metaphor of a nail. It says that however hard you may try, it is very difficult to pull out a nail that has been hammered into a plank, but you can push it out to the other side by hammering in another nail on top of it. This metaphor teaches how a person cannot have two different emotions at the same time. You cannot have both negative and positive thoughts at the same time. This is one of the basic Truths that I taught at the early stage of our development.

It is actually very hard to live positively while having dark and depressing thoughts. As in the metaphor of the nail I just mentioned, hammering a new nail on top of the nail in the plank pushes the first nail out. So, it is essential to change, as quickly as possible, your dark or depressed feelings to the opposite way of thinking.

When you are constantly in a depressed state, you may feel miserable. But you are also taking love in many ways from various people who are in contact with you, such as your family, colleagues at work and other people connected with you in your life. The problem is that you, yourself, do not realize that. And the more people try to comfort you, the more you behave like a tragic hero or heroine, soaking up their love. You have no idea that you are actually becoming a burden to others; you just believe yourself to be so pure that you can get hurt easily.

In life, we make many mistakes. Many things do not go as we wish.

Sometimes we may find that what we believed to be common sense is different from the accepted knowledge of society. You may find that your convictions are not in accord with your company's conventions. But if you find that you have hammered in a nail of failure, you need to hammer in a new nail of positive thinking on top to push that first one out. To put it another way, you need to overcome negativity with positivity. For example, if something happens to make you feel down, try tackling the issue from a different angle. This way of thinking made it much easier for me to handle things.

### *Sublimate jealousy and a sense of inferiority, Turning them into positive energy*

There is yet another important endeavor to become someone attractive: overcoming jealousy and an inferiority complex. I, too, used to have these feelings when I was young.

Many people are likely to develop feelings of jealousy or inferiority in their school days. Nowadays, some may start to develop such feelings during their elementary school days. In elementary, junior high and high school, jealousy can arise from things such as differences in academic ability, athletic ability, popularity with the opposite sex, or friendliness. A great many people may still carry this inferiority complex into adulthood.

In school, you will also find other people who you feel are more fortunate than you are. For example, there are those who are good at studies, fluent in a second language, or have a flattering figure.

Some people are from a rich family and may talk about their luxury summer vacation in Switzerland, for instance. Being unable to afford travel abroad, you may find their words irritating. If you find four or five others who think like you, you may want to get together and bully that person. Some people may find it unbearable to hear that their rich classmates have a holiday home in Switzerland, and may actually start bullying them.

You can easily harbor jealousy and a sense of inferiority in everyday situations like these, but you must somehow overcome them. Such feelings are not confined to your school days but will continue into adulthood. If you compare yourself with others, you will continue to feel jealous or inferior. Unless you overcome this, you will unfortunately become an unattractive person who other people would not want to be like.

Successful people are good at sublimating these feelings of jealousy and inferiority, and turning them into positive energy they can use. They are very skillful in doing this; this is one of the distinctive traits of successful people.

## *Use your inferiority complex as a principle of courage*
## *To inspire other people*

Some people can use their feelings of inferiority as a principle of courage to inspire others. The founder of Panasonic, Konosuke Matsushita,* for example, did not hide that he did not graduate from elementary school but instead mentioned it repeatedly. A man without an elementary school education founded and grew his company, gradually employing high school graduates, then technical college graduates, then university graduates, and eventually engineers who graduated from top-tier universities. It may seem strange, but he achieved this without hiding his educational background. Jealousy or inferiority is a natural feeling to have in his case, but instead, he esteemed his employees and was grateful that so many talented people had come to work for him.

In another more recent case, Kazuo Inamori† was a similar type of person. He failed the exam to enter Kagoshima Junior High School in the prewar education system, and later again he failed the exam to enter Osaka University. Apparently, he was not good at studying during his school years, and even when looking for employment, he failed to get hired at most of the large electrical

---

* Konosuke Matsushita [1894 – 1989] was a well-known Japanese industrialist who started his own business in 1918 and developed it to eventually become the present-day Panasonic, one of the largest Japanese multinational electronics companies. He is often referred to as a "god of management" in Japan for his business philosophy.

† Kazuo Inamori [1932 -] is a well-known Japanese industrialist, who founded and developed two major Japanese companies, Kyocera and KDDI. At the age of 78, he was asked by the government to revive Japan Airlines, and successfully turned it around from bankruptcy in just three years.

appliance manufacturers of the day. So, he joined a company that none of his friends and acquaintances had ever heard of. Eventually, however, after a number of years of hard work at the company, he left to start his own business with several others who followed him, and was able to expand it. That was the predecessor to the multinational electronics and ceramics manufacturer Kyocera. Mr. Inamori also created the telecommunications operator DDI, which became today's KDDI, and in recent years he is noted for having taken on the task of reviving Japan Airlines Co. [JAL].

He also openly reveals that he had an inferiority complex and humbly says, "If someone like me could achieve this success, it would be perfectly natural for people brighter than myself to achieve even more success." In this way, he shows us a principle of courage. Someone who has managed to achieve great success, viewed from an objective and social standpoint, can transform his or her past experience into an inspiring story.

Revealing one's inferiority complex can be a mere self-depreciating act if done before one attains great success, so it is quite difficult to say how much you should reveal. But if skillfully used, such negative emotions can serve in a positive way, like the starting block for the 100-meter dash; you can create a surge of speed by pushing against it. In the same way, try to use inferiority or jealousy as a springboard to turn your life into something positive.

# 6

# Characteristics of
# Attractive People

✧    ✧    ✧

*The more your success is self-earned, the more you feel*
*Appreciation for those around you*

So, how can you make up for your inferiority complex or jealousy, and turn it into your asset? This requires effort on your part. A path will rarely open in a good direction for those who do not make efforts.

As you concentrate your effort in opening up a way forward, your feelings will gradually change. Instead of attributing all your success to your own hard work, you will begin to think that your success is due to the people around you, or God or Buddha. It is truly ironic, but people who built themselves up and became successful through their own efforts will tend to be more thankful for other factors, such as their luck, God's power, and support from other people.

On the other hand, those who make no efforts to improve themselves and have no experience of success as a result of self-effort tend to blame other people or their environment for their failure and cannot move forward from there. These people are basically not so likable; rather, they are probably disliked. This is a crucial point.

Even if you have achieved success through your own hard

efforts, you will gradually develop a tendency to focus more on other people's support while focusing less on your own effort. This means you have developed humility.

## *Chase after a big dream and stay humble at the same time*

In a sense, you need to be ambitious in order to be someone attractive. Especially when you are young, talk ambitiously about your big dreams. That is more attractive.

However, it is no good if your overconfidence becomes a nuisance to those around you. You need to stay humble even as you remain ambitious and speak of your big dreams. Constantly chasing after big dreams and staying humble may seem contradictory, but you need to make efforts to manage these feelings and balance the two. I truly believe this is the kind of person who will eventually become an attractive person.

## *North Korea and China are showing us good examples Of unattractive behavior*

Conversely, what about the people who are unattractive? If you take someone unattractive to mean someone disliked, you can see such examples in clips of North Korean Central Television [KCTV] broadcasts sometimes shown on the news and other TV programs. These clips clearly show how people come to be disliked.

They say nothing but bad things about the other party; they do not even think about the other party's position. They simply continue to assert their own position, saying that they are the only ones who are right. You will certainly be disliked if you act like that. They ceaselessly do this in their state-run broadcasts.

The Chinese foreign minister and press secretary also act in the same manner. They go on and on with their one-sided arguments; I wonder if they are aware that acting like that will only cause everyone to dislike them. They might be able to brainwash their own citizens with such broadcasts, but not the people outside the country. Those who enjoy freedom will not be brainwashed in that way.

The Chinese and North Koreans do not seem to understand that such tricks will not work on people who have the freedom to argue back. They convey information that makes me wonder if they truly believe they can control foreign people in the same way that they do their own citizens. They are actually showing us examples of unattractive behavior. I feel that they need to take a careful look at their own issues.

Japan, on the other hand, overly deprecates itself. So, Japanese people need to recognize their own good points a little more.

Happy Science is engaged in political activities, too, so we also need to check and see whether or not our activities are becoming like KCTV broadcasts. We must carefully judge whether or not we are simply asserting our own position and constantly criticizing other parties. It is important to avoid being overly one-sided. A little kindness or consideration will do.

## *Attractive people are those who have accomplished things With conviction*

In this chapter, I have talked in various ways about how to become an attractive person. My ultimate message is this: stay firm in your conviction and follow through with things to the end.

Your conviction should not be based on your desire for self-preservation; it must bring happiness to people of the world and truly guide society in the right direction. Those with such conviction and who have actually accomplished their goal are truly attractive.

There are many different paths, but whatever path you take, have a strong conviction, withstand various criticisms, and do what is right while also reflecting upon your thoughts and deeds. This is essential. In this endeavor, you will find that even people who initially criticized you will eventually turn into your fans.

# WHAT IS MISSIONARY WORK?

*The starting point of religious activities*
*Is summarized by the words,*
*"Missionary work."*
*What is missionary work?*
*It means, "To tell the Way."*
*Then, what is "the Way" we must tell others?*
*It is the Path*
*Which we, as human beings, should walk.*
*It is the Way to the Truth.*

*Many people cannot even recognize*
*The path they should walk*
*Because they are not taught the Way to the Truth,*
*And they walk on a wrong path.*
*They believe they are walking*
*On a flat and easy road,*
*Enjoying a comfortable journey,*
*When in fact they are descending*
*Into a deep valley,*
*Sinking into the muddy marshes,*
*Or falling down a steep cliff into the sea.*

*This is the reality*
*Seen from the spiritual perspective,*
*From the perspective of the Truth.*
*Many people do not realize*
*They are now walking a dangerous path,*
*Or that an unfortunate future awaits them*
*In several decades and beyond*
*Because they see things*
*Only through their physical eyes.*
*However, through spiritual eyes,*
*Or from the perspective of the Real World,*
*It is as clear as day*
*Which is the Way to the Truth,*
*The straightforward path, the right path,*
*And which is the path*
*That leads people's lives to destruction.*

*The right way is revealed by the Truth*
*Taught only by true religions,*
*And it can by no means be shown*
*By any academic discipline,*
*Education, or philosophy.*
*Therein lies the true mission of religion.*

From *The Heart of Mission*

Chapter THREE

# The Starting Point for Human Happiness

*The Importance of Faith and a Religious Mind*

# 1

## The Importance of Faith
## And a Religious Mind

✧　　✧　　✧

*Happy Science has celebrated the 35th anniversary*
*Of the Great Enlightenment and the*
*30th anniversary of its founding*

The year 2016 was a significant year for Happy Science, marking the 35th anniversary of the Great Enlightenment and the 30th anniversary of its founding. As three decades have now passed since our founding, I believe that we have, to a certain extent, established our position as an influential religious group in Japan, and we are becoming known around the world. If we totaled the number of people overseas who know about Happy Science, it would most probably be much bigger than the number in Japan, though our activities overseas are still vigorously in progress.

I do not know how well known my birthplace, Tokushima Prefecture, is overseas, but I believe that one day Tokushima will become a holy land for the world. In March 2016, we released the movie, *I'm Fine, My Angel* [executive producer: Ryuho Okawa], and on that occasion we announced the establishment of Holy Land El Cantare Seitankan in my birth town of Kawashima, Yoshinogawa City in Tokushima, to commemorate the 30th anniversary of our founding. I feel a little embarrassed to build such a facility in my birth town, but I thought it would be a good idea to have something that would mark our presence for the future. I believe it will become a pilgrimage site for visitors from all over the world.

Tokushima is well known for its Awa Dance Festival, but in the near future, I believe a variety of people will visit there from around the world, not just for the Awa Dance Festival, but also for various events centered around my birthday on July 7. So, the future of Tokushima is certainly very bright. With this preamble, I intend to focus on religious topics in this chapter.

## *The question that bewildered the spirit of former Prime Minister Takeo Miki, who was from Tokushima Prefecture*

This chapter is the transcript of the lecture I gave on April 23, 2016, in Tokushima. Before giving the lecture, I thought I should collect some of the latest information about the Spirit World in connection to Tokushima, so two days before my lecture, I summoned the spirit of Takeo Miki, the only prime minister to have come from Tokushima, to Happy Science. His messages are recorded as "Spiritual Messages from Takeo Miki" [recorded on April 21, 2016].

In the first half of his message, he spoke quite logically, giving me the impression that he was a great figure, but in the latter half I found that he was not really familiar with details of the Spirit World; I felt he was still very lacking in knowledge. When asked why he chose to be born in Tokushima, he was momentarily at a loss for words and did not seem to know how to respond. Apparently, the questioner's intention was to ask him whether he had a significant mission to fulfill as he was born in Tokushima prior to my birth. If he had been born after me, he probably would have known why he was being asked such a question, but he didn't know how to respond because the order of our births was the reverse. I remember him being at a loss for an answer.

If I were asked why I was born in Tokushima, I would most probably answer that it was because Shikoku Island, in which Tokushima is located, has been a protected spiritual ground for more than a thousand years, ever since the Japanese Buddhist monk Kobo Daishi Kukai* established the pilgrimage route through the 88 temples. We receive great cultural influence from the environment in which we were born and raised, so having such a spiritual environment was the major reason why I chose that place.

---

* Kukai [774 - 835], who founded esoteric Shingon Sect of Buddhism, is said to have possessed the powers of clairvoyance and clairaudience, and was able to communicate with the spirits of the Real World. Born in Kagawa Prefecture in Shikoku, he spent his younger days undergoing spiritual training in various places in Shikoku, some of which are now known as the 88 pilgrimage sites.

## Today's academics and science do not Acknowledge spiritual matters

Being born and raised in such a faithful environment did not solve all problems, of course. The greater part of my life involved the process of overcoming the inner conflict that arose from growing up in such a rural area and then studying and working in a city environment. Shikoku is not really an advantageous location if one wants to gain a comprehensive view of world affairs and of Japan as a whole. But experiencing the gap between the pure faithfulness of my birthplace and the direction in which Japan and the world are heading has greatly served me to think about what needs to be done. It gave me tremendous learning opportunities.

I grew up in Tokushima and eventually moved to Tokyo. In Tokyo, I found that the commonly accepted knowledge was very different from that of Tokushima. Simply put, people in Tokyo were not very receptive to open talk of spiritual matters such as faith and the other world. My words seemed to slide off them, like drops of water rolling off an oiled cloth. I found this attitude in the field of academics and the field of science, as well as in urban cultures. I also felt that this was strongly the case in other developed countries outside Japan.

To expound on this further, I could say the following: Nowadays, terms such as the Spirit World, the other world, God, Buddha, higher spirit, bodhisattvas and tathagatas are nearly extinct in the academic world and are considered non-existent. The prevailing trend now is to believe that the goals of humankind are to make the earthly lives more comfortable and convenient, and to live happily just in the world that we can see. Although there are various academic disciplines and specializations, they all have the viewpoint that what is happening on the surface of Earth is all there is. When looking at the universe, too, the majority of people feel that the universe that can be seen through a telescope is everything that exists, and they believe that this viewpoint is "enlightened."

## The "faith" of post-war Japanese society Is at the level of believing in a fortune

In April 2016, I published the spiritual messages from Japanese former Prime Minister Takeo Fukuda [See, *Jiminto Shokun ni Tsugu—Fukuda Takeo no Reigen* (literally, "A Spiritual Message from Takeo Fukuda, Addressing the Members of the LDP"), (Tokyo: The Happy Science Institute of Government and Management, 2016)]. In the preface, I noted that a survey conducted in the United States showed that about 98% of the people responded "yes" to the question that simply asked, "Do you believe in God?" Although results may differ depending on how surveys are conducted, in the U.S., almost 98% of the people say they believe in God, and only 2% do not.

In Japan, on the other hand, a little more than 10% of the people would answer "yes" to the same question; it is closer to 15% or 16%. If the question is direct, less than 20% answer that they believe in God. But if questions are phrased in a different manner, such as, "Do you visit a shrine during the New Year?," "Do you visit your family tomb during the annual season?," "Do you believe in the power of amulets?," or "Do you sometimes want to have a purification rite performed by a Shinto priest?," then more than half of them reply that they do.

They say they do not believe in God or Buddha, but they carry around amulets for success or for traffic safety. I don't see the point in carrying around such things if there were no God or Buddha, but they seem to have some shallow belief, at the level of believing in a fortune. Apparently, this level of faith is compatible in keeping up with the advancements in this modern world. This is the commonly accepted attitude in Japan today, though it is far from the world standard.

However, it has not always been the case in Japan. This trend became extremely apparent after World War II. Ever since the postwar constitution separated church and state, religion was divorced from school education and has been treated as a kind of superstition, but it was not the case before then. In fact, the 70 or so years since WWII have been an anomaly. Prewar Japanese were more like Americans today; if asked about their religious beliefs, around 98% of them would have affirmed the existence of God and Buddha as a matter of course.

Just because a country has lost a war, it does not mean that all its values were mistaken. I want to say that there is no need to be so self-tormenting. Victory or defeat can be experienced in a material civilization, but it is too extreme to repudiate all the traditions that had existed until then or to destroy everything that was previously believed. There has to be a proper reaction to restore such values.

## *Our publishing of hundreds of spiritual messages reveals Differences in character between the spirits*

Happy Science has continued its activities for 30 years with an aim to inspire people to regain faith. I have given numerous lectures and written many books on theory. I have also published a great number of spiritual messages [over 400 books as of November 2016]. Some people say that there is no need to publish such collections of spiritual messages, and that teaching my own ideas is good enough. I used to think like that myself, and there was a period of more than 10 years when I did not publish any new spiritual messages.

As the years passed, however, there was an increasing number of young people with no knowledge of spiritual messages. They are astonished to hear about the other world, that people retain their personality even after they die. They believe that the brain is the true nature of the soul, and that everything ends with the cessation of brain activity. More and more people think like this and accept it as a matter of course.

A great many people believe that souls and the afterlife are mere perceptions created by the brain and nervous system. But what if, after a body has been cremated or buried, one's ability to think actually remains? If so, those beliefs will be proven wrong.

That is why I am putting many collections of spiritual messages out into the world.

Sometimes the ideas of spirits are different from my own. Everyone has his or her own characteristic way of thinking, so naturally some of them differ from mine. In this regard, publishing their ideas makes it difficult for me to create a uniform set of teachings, but I have dared to publish many spiritual messages in order to show people the difference in the various spirits' character retained in the other world even after death, just as each person has a different character in this world.

The truth is this: you are born into this world, and live a number of decades before eventually returning to the other world. When you die, you are cremated and placed in a grave, but that is not the end. The spiritual messages prove this truth; their significance is truly great.

### Faith has the power to make this world a better place

If everything ends with death after being cremated or placed in a grave, it would be natural for you to live your remaining days comfortably and egoistically to your own satisfaction. But what if death was not the end? If you consider your way of life from this perspective, your life will completely transform.

To take it a step further, this is the same as telling you, as the older people used to say, "Your deceased grandparents are watching over you" or "God and Buddha are watching your life."

The majority of people nowadays would probably laugh at hearing such statements, but what if those statements were true? If people truly believe that God, Buddha, or their deceased grandparents are actually watching over them for the whole of their lives, they would find it very hard to do anything they knew to be wrong.

The same holds true for children. When there is only one sales clerk working in a convenience store late at night, junior high or high school students might think that no one would notice if they snuck a couple of items into their pockets. But if they suddenly thought, "Maybe grandfather is watching me" or "Buddha would certainly not overlook this," that could serve to stop them from shoplifting.

This in fact is the power of faith. Faith actually has the power to make this world a better place and move it forward in the moral sense. By believing that a spiritual being closely connected to you is watching over you, or a being is watching your whole life from another world even when there is actually no one around, you can correct your way of life.

Of course, life would be difficult with no freedom; you would feel totally exposed, as if you are being watched on a surveillance camera. So, these beings are made to be undetectable and you can live believing no one is watching what you are doing. But I am sure you have sometimes sensed the presence of a being spiritually, or heard about such religious truths from your parents or relatives. At such times, you may suddenly become aware of the existence of spiritual beings. It is essential to always be mindful of such presence. In this sense, faith and a religious mind are very important.

# 2

# What Separates Good from Evil

✧   ✧   ✧

### *I talk with ghosts every day,*
### *But horror movies still scare me*

There are many stories about spiritual or religious matters that are popular today, but unfortunately, many of them contain elements that frighten people. I converse with beings from the other world and record their spiritual messages almost every day. So, you might imagine that someone like me would not be frightened by beings of the other world. Officially, I am not; I am not in the least bit scared.

However, even I get scared when I watch a horror movie like *The Ring*, *Spiral*, *One Missed Call*, or *The Exorcist*. I cannot help but get scared; shivers run down my spine. Then, I suddenly realize that I should not be scared by such movies since I converse with ghosts on a daily basis. Those who make such movies intend to scare people. Although they may have heard stories about spirits, they do not really know much about them. So, I sometimes calm myself thinking that I should not get scared when I watch movies that such people have created, because I talk with beings of the other world every day.

But I am not saying that such movies are no good. When I am working, there are times when I feel overwhelmed by the difficulties of teaching people the Truth. At such times, a horror movie, despite being fiction, gives me fresh determination to fight against darkness. In this regard, we cannot say horror movies have absolutely no value.

## *Expelling demons requires Dharma power that Comes with enlightenment*

Generally, in movies about exorcism, exorcists officially certified by the Vatican are easily defeated when they battle against demons. Those characters end up dying by throwing themselves out the window or being pushed down the stairs; it makes me frustrated how weak and pathetic they are.

I have battled against many demons myself, and I am certainly not weak like the exorcists in the movies. You may be able to watch recorded videos of my practicing exorcisms at local Happy Science temples. Usually, it just takes a few seconds for me to expel demons. This is rather easy; I just order them to leave and they are gone in an instant.*

There is a huge difference between the powers of demons and mine; it is not like how it is shown in the movies. In the movies, the Vatican-certified exorcists read the Bible in Latin, hold up a crucifix and sprinkle holy water around, but the demons laugh at them and refuse to leave the person they have possessed. However, Dharma

---

*When there is a need to record a spiritual message from a demon, Ryuho Okawa makes the demon enter a spiritual expert's body and lets it speak, but as soon as the session is over, he expels it in a few seconds. Refer to *Exorcist Nyumon* [literally, "Introduction to Exorcism"] (Tokyo: IRH Press, 2010).

power comes with true enlightenment, and with this power you can expel evil spirits and demons.

Those who have attained enlightenment and put the Truth into practice on a daily basis develop a kind of spiritual power. Just as meditative power is acquired through the continual practice of meditation, you can develop various spiritual powers according to the kind of training you undergo.

The esoteric teachings of the Japanese Buddhist monk, Kobo Daishi Kukai, have been popular on Shikoku Island. His life was most probably a life of an exorcist. He must have performed various kinds of exorcisms, and I understand this very well.

### *Whether you wish for others' happiness or Unhappiness will determine the direction You are heading*

Spirits who are unable to return to Heaven after death, such as those who died in traffic accidents or from sudden illness, are often seen by people, but this is not surprising at all. The problem is the other spirits in the background that try to draw the spirits of the newly deceased down to Hell, or send them to homes to bring misfortune, causing even greater unhappiness and destroying those families. There really are such spirits; they plot and make plans to manipulate others from behind. I sometimes confront these spirits. Their wrongdoings must not be allowed to continue.

Sometimes we need to accept our own unhappiness, but there are people in the world who, when they cannot find happiness, take delight in making other people unhappy and mocking them. For example, someone unsuccessful in making money might relish seeing other people fail financially or go bankrupt, saying, "Serves you right!" Or, someone who is unable to recover from an illness could be relieved to hear that his neighbor has died of cancer. There are people like this, who feel good or feel they can forgive others upon seeing those people's misfortunes. However, you need to know that these kinds of feelings are the worst as a human being.

Sometimes you cannot be happy because of circumstances outside your control, such as your environment or the current political system. It may be that you have not been blessed with a family life. But sometimes there are reasons for your not having been blessed with a good life or for not being happy at this moment. You need to consider these reasons well, too. If your sense of misery leads you toward wishing for the unhappiness of others, your mind will be attuned to that of evil spirits and demons. This needs to be noted.

The principle is simple. It is not very difficult. Do you wish for the happiness of other people, or do you wish for their unhappiness? The direction your feelings are inclined will determine the course of your life and afterword.

To put it more simply, those who have spent decades of their lives wishing for the happiness of other people will basically return to Heaven. When such people die, the angels and bodhisattvas in the other world will be sure to come and guide them to the place they deserve.

On the other hand, there are also people who, during their lifetime, wished for others' unhappiness and were actually working to support the wrongdoings of evil spirits and demons. They may have bullied other people, for example, which was also featured in our movie, *I'm Fine, My Angel.** Some people take pleasure in joining in acts of bullying, despite being well aware that they should not be doing so. There are also people who try to protect themselves with cowardly attitudes, joining a gang of bullies, so that they will not become the next target. These two types of people are the same; they are drawn in the direction of wishing for the unhappiness of others.

Basically, good or evil is determined in this way. Do you choose to help realize the happiness of others? Do you want to form your life so as to bring happiness to other people? Do you want to lead this type of life? Do you want this type of work? Or, conversely, are you content with a life of wishing unhappiness on other people? The path forks here into two directions. Looked at individually, there are cases with more details involved, of course. But roughly speaking, these are the two orientations.

---

*The movie features five short stories, one of which is about an 11-year-old girl who was bullied by her friends, but successfully overcame the situation with guidance from an angel.

## *Increase the number of people on earth*
## *Who wish for the happiness of others*

Happy Science is aiming to make humankind happy, but what do we mean by that? We are actually trying to increase the number of people on earth who wish for the expansion of others' happiness.

Do not be drawn into making society worse or causing unhappiness for others, telling yourself that it is perfectly natural to feel like that. Humans possess an animalistic nature, or animal instincts, and it is only natural to think of protecting oneself or of undermining others. Animals are all filled with fear. Their basic fears are of being eaten and of starving to death. It is almost impossible for them to break free from these two fears. Their lives are dominated by the fear of starvation, the fear of being eaten, and the fear of being killed. These fears are also spreading in the world of humans.

However, humans are on a higher level than animals. So, we must have a clear sense of good and evil. On an individual, case-by-case basis, it can be difficult to determine good or evil, but generally speaking, as I just said, it is a matter of whether you lead other people in a direction that will bring them happiness or unhappiness. Please think carefully about this in your daily life. This is the starting point of determining good and evil.

# 3

# Thinking About Political Issues from the Standpoint of Religion

### *A top official of the Democratic Party of Japan said, "Protect the lives of the Self-Defense Force members!"*

Looking at individual cases, however, there are also tough issues in determining good and evil. The majority of religious groups in Japan now advocate such political issues as anti-war, peace and environmental conservation, and support activities to promote these issues. This is true of the majority of Buddhist monks, Christian priests, as well as those in new religious groups.

Slogans such as "Anti-war," "Peace," "Environmental conservation" and "Protect the Okinawan dugong [marine mammal]" do indeed sound nice, and it feels good to make such appeals. On the other hand, with regard to the national security bills that the Japanese government recently passed that would allow Japan and the U.S. to carry out joint military exercises, these same groups call those bills "war bills" and say that such bills are not favorable because Japan could be drawn into war.*

---

*Japan's new security laws were enacted on September 30, 2015, and came into effect on March 29, 2016.

The new chair of the Democratic Party's Policy Research Committee once said that we must protect the lives of Self-Defense Force members. When I heard that, I almost fell over in shock; I could not believe my ears for a moment, and thought, "What? Aren't the Self-Defense Force members supposed to be protecting the lives of the Japanese people?"

In the world, there are jobs that entail the risk of losing one's life. Firefighting is one of them. But what if, for example, someone stood in front of fire trucks during a fire, strongly insisting to protect the lives of the firefighters? People in general would say, "What are you saying? Their job is to put out fires, isn't it? The firefighters' job is to risk their lives to save people from burning buildings." In this way, most people would find it odd to hear someone insisting on the protection of the lives of firefighters and stopping them from carrying out their jobs.

The same is true with the police. If there were a campaign to protect the lives of police officers, then they would not be sent anywhere dangerous. Suppose a robber with a knife broke into a person's house, and the person called the police. If a police officer answered that he was too scared to respond, he would not be doing his job. We can only say that he is nothing more than a parasite living off our taxes. Thus, there are actually jobs that involve putting one's own life on the line to protect other people.

## *People involved in religion must not be Mistaken about evil*

You could say the same thing about those involved in religion. As I mentioned earlier, some people are unable to return to Heaven after they die. It is a common occurrence and we must save their souls. But besides that, there are also people with evil ambitions. If these people are deteriorating the world, we must take action in tangible ways to stop them from fulfilling their ambitions. To do this, the power of an individual alone is not sufficient; we need the collective power of many people. We need to concentrate the will of many people to alter the direction in which the world is heading.

Religious people must not be mistaken on this point. Please consider things carefully. Many people advocate peace and environmental conservation, and those involved in religion tend to strongly insist on such matters, too. I would endorse them if that were the right direction. However, if, as a result of doing this, people ultimately become cowardly, indifferent to others' happiness and simply does what appeals to their hearts, then that is a problem. Religious people must be wiser in this respect.

## *Frequent earthquakes are signs That the country is in disarray*

Earthquakes are another topic that is very much on people's minds at the moment, but this, too, is a very difficult issue. When an earthquake strikes, people are killed and the victims seek help. Helping those people is certainly a heroic action that no one would oppose. Happy Science, too, has repeatedly taken action such as providing hot meals and supplying clean water. This is a perfectly natural reaction, and should not be the target of criticism.

Nevertheless, I have an objection to those who take the causes of such disasters solely in materialistic terms and say, "Earthquakes occur because there are faults." Japan has had numerous faults since olden times. So, the issue is, "Why are they becoming more active now?" Happy Science is now exploring this point.

Roughly 10% of the world's earthquakes occur in the Japanese archipelago, and we cannot prevent earthquakes altogether. However, having looked into the past, we find that there have been many earthquakes during periods when the country was in disarray.

When a country is in disarray, disasters such as earthquakes, tsunamis, volcanic eruptions and epidemics become prevalent. At such times, various religious leaders emerge to give new teachings. Or in the political world, revolutions occur and governments are overthrown and replaced by new powers. Many such things happen when the heavens are not happy with humans.

## *The Japan-related gods are pressing Japan for its renovation*

In Japan, there has been a series of major earthquakes in recent years, starting from the Great Hanshin-Awaji Earthquake in 1995, and then the Great East Japan Earthquake in 2011, with the Kumamoto Earthquake in 2016. During these 20 to 25 years, the Japanese economy has been in a period of stagnation. These events reflect the fact that the heavens are not very happy about the current state of Japan. It is clear that the Japan-related gods do not really approve of the current situation of Japan.

I feel that they are probably frustrated with Japan's attitude of abandoning its mission to further develop powerfully and take a position as a world leader. That is why they are pressing for Japan's renovation. That is the spiritual information that we have been receiving.

Regarding Happy Science, they are scolding us, "You founded Happy Science 30 years ago, but you're still at this level? Your progress is too slow. What have you been doing?" I feel like I am being told, "Is this all you could do in these 30 years? We thought you could do more to better the world, but you haven't gotten very far." I feel responsible for this situation. There needs to be a much more powerful surge of our activities, and unless such a force expands throughout Japan, we cannot reach the whole world. There are no words to describe this bitterness of regret in face of this reality.

## There should be "El Cantare Airport" In Tokushima Prefecture

Recently, many earthquakes are occurring due to the active faults in the Oita and Kumamoto areas in Kyushu. The Median Tectonic Line stretches from Kyushu to as far as the Matsuyama City in Ehime Prefecture and close to Yoshinogawa City in Tokushima Prefecture, on Shikoku Island. So, some people in Shikoku may be scared, imagining that Shikoku might be torn in half, should earthquakes strike along the fault in those regions.

But hold it right there. Shikoku is my birthplace. I would not let such things happen! From now on, I intend to spread the basic teachings and thoughts of Happy Science to the entire world, and make the energy circulate to bring happiness to humankind. Shikoku is the central or pivotal place to do so. It is the place of origin for Happy Science, my birthplace, which I metaphorically consider my cradle. However, I am at a loss for words to think that we might have a weak foothold in this area.

In neighboring Kochi Prefecture, for example, there is "Kochi Ryoma Airport," commemorating the birthplace of Ryoma Sakamoto [1836 - 1867], one of the prominent samurai leaders of the Meiji Restoration. Tokushima presently has Tokushima Awaodori Airport, but I do not see why it needs to be named after the Awa dance. I can see nothing wrong with it being named, "Tokushima El Cantare Airport"; people around the world would find it easier to understand.

I must say that our believers in Tokushima or the entire island of Shikoku are slightly lacking in strength unless they are strongly determined to make it happen. I would be very happy if I could receive stronger support from the place where I was born and raised. I am from Tokushima in Shikoku and I certainly do not want to think about anything that would be disadvantageous to my birthplace; however, I am very sad that I have yet to gain sufficient trust from the people there.

I give many lectures, and among them the Celebration of the Lord's Descent in July and the El Cantare Celebration in December are now broadcast on six or seven local TV stations. However, they are still not shown in the area where I was born, and residents there can only view them via Wakayama TV [the nearest local TV station from Tokushima]. I have the impression that our activities are not yet so active in my hometown area. I would like our believers to show the true strength of our home ground. The Japanese religious group Tenrikyo was strong enough to have established Tenri City in Nara Prefecture, Japan, so I hope we could see a similar kind of strength in our home ground.

# 4

# Missionary Work Offers Others a Chance To be Saved and an Opportunity to Awaken to the Truth

✧   ✧   ✧

### Leap over the boundary between this world and The other, and grasp the Truth

Let me summarize my main message. First, we must confirm the Truth. School education is generally based on the idea that humans are nothing more than physical bodies that can be seen. Therefore, with school education alone, people in this world would not be able to know whether humans are mere physical existences or whether they are endowed with souls. However, teaching morality based on the idea that humans are merely physical existences is no different from teaching traffic regulations; there is no spirituality.

One needs to be taught about the world of truth in order to raise his or her spirituality. For this reason, it is extremely important that educators as well as those with higher ranks in society have the right faith. I especially want people in such higher positions to study about the world of truth and gain proper knowledge of it. I want intellectuals to study about it as well.

Contemporary academic principles are mainly based on

skepticism and see this skepticism as the scientific approach. In journalism, too, there is a strong tendency to try to reach the Truth through doubt upon doubt. However, doubting is not the only way to attain the Truth. In some ways, Truth cannot be truly attained without a leap of faith.

A barrier lies between this world and the other world, so inevitably, we have to take a leap. We must leap across the gap or valley that lies there. Unless you dare to leap across it, you cannot truly grasp the Truth. That is what it means to have faith. You need to make that leap at some point in life.

Nevertheless, the valley appears to be very wide, and the fear of falling makes people unable to leap. This is the state of average people. As this world contaminates their perspective, they increasingly feel that taking the leap is very difficult and fear that something frightening will happen on the other side. However, once you have confidence in the Truth, you must hold onto it firmly.

### *Shakyamuni Buddha and I both have the ability to see The past, present and future*

The Truth has been lost in academic learning, but this is not only true of materialistic study that deals with objects; studies of religion and Buddhism have also lost it. They have become akin to philosophy. The teachings of Shakyamuni Buddha preached more than 2,500 years ago have become a kind of philosophy that man ponders and interprets only intellectually.

Even the Buddhist universities in Japan teach students in this manner. They teach the formality of Buddhist practice, such as how to sit in meditation or chant the prayers, but there is no substance in it because they do not believe in any of the substance. They believe, for example, that Shakyamuni Buddha simply spent time in mediation like a yoga practitioner, and therefore leading a simple life in meditation is good enough. Quite a few think this way.

However, this way of thinking is mistaken. It is certainly true that Shakyamuni Buddha did spend time in meditation and concentration, but if we take a look at his entire life we can see that there is much more substance there. In Buddhist scriptures, it is clearly written that Shakyamuni Buddha gained *sammyo* [three kinds of spiritual wisdom] when he attained enlightenment beneath the Bodhi tree.

The three kinds of spiritual wisdom mean the three kinds of ability: the ability to see the past, the ability to see the present and the ability to see the future. It is clearly written in Buddhist scriptures that when he attained enlightenment he could see the past, present and future. That is the meaning of having gained the three kinds of spiritual wisdom.

Let me explain them, one by one. First, what does it mean to be able to see the past? At Happy Science local branches and shojas [temples], you can see videos of my conducting past-life readings. On those occasions, I do a reading [spiritual research] on the subject's past life and the lives before that, and clarify the kind of karma he or she possesses. Sometimes we find that a woman in this life was a man in a previous life, or vice versa, or learn what the person did in his or her past lives. I see the entire past in this way.

Then, I consider how the past is influencing the person now. For instance, if the person is experiencing problems at home or with relatives, I can clearly see the spiritual influences at work or the underlying reasons for his or her problems. This is the ability to see the present.

I can also see the trend of world affairs. For example, I can view the thoughts of China's Xi Jinping. As a religious leader, I have the ability to see through what Mr. Xi Jinping is thinking now [see, *Sekai Kotei wo Mezasu Otoko* (literally, "The Man Aspiring to Become the World Emperor") (Tokyo: IRH Press, 2010), and *China's Hidden Agenda: A Spiritual Interview with Xi Jinping* (Tokyo: HS Press, 2012)], as well as what Mr. Donald Trump is thinking [see, *The Trump Secret: Seeing Through the Past, Present and Future of the New American President* (New York: IRH Press, 2017)]. I am able to read other people's minds.

In addition, I also have the ability to see the future and I can read how the future will unfold. Once I read the future, I consider whether what I have seen is an acceptable way of life or future for humankind. If I decide it is not right, I must give teachings to change the direction of the future. I must present new ways of thinking and say, "Aim to move in this direction," or "Change your ways of thinking in this way." These are the three kinds of spiritual wisdom that Shakyamuni Buddha is said to have acquired when he attained enlightenment.

## *Shakyamuni Buddha acquired the six divine powers And was able to perform remote-viewing*

Shakyamuni Buddha is also said to have acquired the six divine powers. These include various abilities, all of which are supernatural powers. It is impossible for someone who has acquired divine powers to ever teach that there are no such things as the other world, God or high spirits, and that everything ends with death. Today's prominent scholars and high-ranking monks have lost sight of this fundamental and obvious fact.

In Shakyamuni Buddha's days, there was no modern transportation system, so he did missionary work as he walked from monastery to monastery. This has now become the style of Buddhist training where monks walk through the mountains. However, they only keep the outward appearance of his act. The same is true for those who practice meditation. They only imitate the form and fail to recognize its true meaning.

So, what exactly did Shakyamuni Buddha experience in his spiritual training? In fact, he performed the rituals to communicate with the Real World by means of meditation. That is how he acquired various new kinds of wisdom, and was able to see people who were hundreds of miles away.

It is recorded in Buddhist scriptures that Shakyamuni Buddha performed remote-viewing after attaining enlightenment under the Bodhi tree: he could see where the five people, who had previously undergone spiritual training with him, were and what they were doing.

At the time, they were at the Deer Park or Magadaava [now known as Sarnath], a well-known place in Buddhism; he could clearly see them even though they were hundreds of miles away. He then set off on foot to go there to give his very first sermon and turn the Wheel of Dharma.

The abilities that I am revealing now, the ones that you are witnessing through my writings and videos, are very similar to those possessed by Shakyamuni Buddha, though there may be some slight differences. For example, I sometimes conduct what we call "space-people readings" to explore the subconscious of living people and read ancient memories of their past lives as space beings. These readings trace back hundreds of millions of years, so they recount things that are far beyond human imagination. It is only natural that some people find them hard to believe.

In Buddhism, the Jataka tales describe various stories of past lives; some stories go far back, to reincarnations of the distant past. Most of them are narrative tales, and we cannot take everything at face value, but Shakyamuni Buddha did talk about many past lives. Based on the result of life-readings, Shakyamuni Buddha taught people, for example, "You have such tendency of the soul as a result of these kinds of lives. That is why you are sick now," "that is why you are experiencing such domestic problems," or "You do not get along with that person now, because you were enemies in a past life. Remember that and try to be friends in this lifetime."

If you re-read Buddha's teachings with that knowledge, you can discover completely new aspects within the teachings.

But even the Japanese Buddhist monks of the 13th century, at a time when various schools of Buddhism were flourishing in Japan, did not really understand that. Kukai, on the other hand, had plenty of spiritual experiences himself, so he may have understood most of the spiritual aspects of those teachings.

## *Spread the Truth to those around you*
## *While you refine your mind*

I would like to explain that there are two kinds of enlightenment. First is the enlightenment as an individual; from the very beginning, you should undergo spiritual training to seek enlightenment as an individual. Strive to attain enlightenment; with that power of enlightenment, purify your mind and enhance your sense of true happiness. This is the kind of spiritual training you will take part in throughout your life.

When you die, you can only take back the mind that you have built up throughout your life. You cannot bring with you all the material things you have made in this world. Your mind is the only thing that you can take with you to the other world. Since it is the only thing you can take back, you need to refine your mind thoroughly and strive daily to advance in the right direction until you go back to the other world. This is the first enlightenment as an individual.

The second enlightenment can be explained as follows: Human beings cannot live alone. Humans are not designed to live on their own but in groups, with many others. There are people who share the same environment as you, who happen to live in the same age, the same region, or work in the same workplace, due to a spiritual connection. This being so, you need to aspire to offer them a chance to be saved and an opportunity to awaken to the Truth.

The act of spreading the Laws or telling the Truth, called missionary work or religious dissemination, is extremely important. Schools do not teach about religious matters. In the older days, homes used to function as a teaching environment as well, but now they have lost that function. They have lost their significance as a place for religious education or education of the souls. We are living in such kind of an era. If schools and homes can no longer teach the Truth, someone will need to guide people in the religious meaning; otherwise, some people will finish their lives without ever encountering the Truth. This needs to be understood.

In addition to striving to improve yourself, help others to awaken to the world of Truth. It is important that those who have awakened to the Truth join hands and take concrete actions to better this world and turn it into a Buddhaland utopia. This is a very important point. Just having this intention in mind is not good enough. Since you have been given a precious opportunity to undergo soul training in this world, you must contribute to creating a utopian society in a tangible way. You need to think about how you should think and live, together with others, to make this world a better place.

# 5

# Aim to Stay Active for Life

✧   ✧   ✧

### *Licensed nursing homes cannot be run*
### *Without tax money*

In April 2016, I watched a TV program on the NHK [Japan Broadcasting Corporation] channel entitled, "NHK Special." It was about bankruptcy in post-retirement years, showing viewers the danger of running out of money in post-retirement years and thus hastening death. It also showed that living with children is not necessarily better because the children must be caregivers for the parents and therefore will no longer be able to work; they would most likely go bankrupt together. I found the content of this program quite questionable.

What is the message the program was ultimately trying to convey? To me, it just suggested that the government should somehow amass tax revenue and invest it into creating more nursing homes because our later years are looking bleak.

The NHK program also dealt with the operation of nursing homes, and stated that unlicensed homes should not be allowed. This was the basic tone of their broadcast. But we need to think about this carefully. It is said that licensed nursing homes cost about 250,000 yen [approx. 2,400 dollars] per month, which is quite expensive.

Not many people can afford it. Meanwhile, unlicensed nursing homes, only charging about 150,000 yen [approx. 1,440 dollars] per month, are criticized as unauthorized facilities. Under the current regulations, however, there is no way a nursing home can be managed profitably.

Since Happy Science is a religious body, we are thinking of creating our own nursing home system, and have recently opened a trial home called, "Golden Temple for Seniors" in Utsunomiya City, Tochigi Prefecture, Japan. But under current regulations, about 70 employees are required to officially open the facility to accommodate 100 residents.* If 70 employees are needed to care for 100 elderly people, there is no way it could be managed. Anyone running a company or even a small business would certainly understand this.

You cannot run a facility with 100 residents using 70 employees without receiving some kind of financial help, so a large amount of subsidies would usually be necessary. In plain terms, the government has created a high standard to open a facility, and is giving subsidies to those that have met that standard. They lament that welfare facilities for the elderly are lacking or that nursery schools are lacking, but they are the ones creating such severe regulations, making it difficult for people to successfully open and run new facilities without subsidies.

---

*Under the current regulations, running a long-term care facility for the elderly requires having at least 40 staff members for 100 elderly people, including nursing care workers, doctors, nutritionists, and administrative staff. Depending on the number of part-time workers and the degree of nursing care provided, the necessary staff often amounts to around 70.

In order to give such subsidies, the government must collect tax money from somewhere. The point is, government officials are thinking only about how to increase their authority. This is truly outrageous. This needs to be considered carefully.

## Government's intentions for approval And licensing are impractical

Happy Science would not be able to run a senior home, either, if we needed 70 staff members to care for 100 residents. There is no way we could. If we needed 7,000 staff members to care for 10,000 people, it would be disastrous; there would have to be 700,000 people working at a senior home for a million people. It would mean that almost all the young people would have to work in that senior home. Then, who would work at other jobs? There would be no one left.

In an extension of this, we can imagine a society where old people are abandoned in the mountains. This could happen in the future society. Or, there could be fines for getting old. We cannot deny the possibility of a policy being implemented to charge people each year once they are over 80, in order to make them desire earlier death.

Government authorities probably had good intentions. They meant well when they first set such regulations, so as to ensure quality caregiving or private rooms for the elderly. These ideas were probably meant well, but in fact were only good on paper. This is a case where a planned economy by the central government goes wrong. This kind of mistake occurs because the people with no experience in management or business make the plans. Even though they have acted in the hope of making things easier for others, they have actually made things much harder. This has happened a lot in many situations, including schools.

Therefore, we need to get rid of all the wasteful aspects in the approval and licensing process, and let the private sector take care of it as much as possible. This is what is required now. Recognize and accept existing needs, and make efforts to fulfill them. I believe it is essential that the government recognize this.

### *Aim to work as long as you can,*
### *And to live well and die well*

I am making efforts to ensure that Happy Science believers are blessed with strong divine protection. I hope they would be able to continue working actively for as long as possible. I do not want them to spend the decades of their twilight years in a hospital, with tubes inserted everywhere. Rather, I want them to stay healthy right up to the end. So, maybe it would be a good idea to compose a new sutra titled, "The Dharma of the Right Mind for Living Well and Dying Well" or something like that [*laughs*] [Happy Science has a fundamental sutra, *Buddha's Teaching: The Dharma of the Right Mind*, given to members who pledge devotion to the Three Treasures].

Some Buddhist groups simply chant their devotion to the Lotus Sutra or the name of Amitabha Buddha. If this is all it takes, I could release a 30-minute CD of me repeatedly chanting, "The Dharma of the Right Mind for Living Well and Dying Well." It might be quite effective [*laughs*].

If things continue as they are now, Japan's finances will go bust and the government definitely will not be able to take care of the elderly. This is obvious. So, you cannot rely on the national or local governments.

You must gradually start exercising to strengthen your body about 10 years before it starts to rust, and strive to acquire knowledge that will be necessary after 10 years. Start preparing and studying around 10 years in advance, so that you can find new employment. This is critical. You must strengthen your mind and body.

In terms of personal relations, elderly people tend to get irritated, annoyed or angry with young people. So, they need to make efforts to "soften" these traits. Young people seem immature to the elderly, which may sometimes make the elderly want to criticize them. This is a common tendency of old people, so I would advise them to recognize this and stop doing it. They are decades ahead in life, so they can just spot faults in young people, but this does not mean that young people are all bad. They were no different some decades ago; they have simply forgotten this fact.

Therefore, when you reach the older stage of life, use your life experiences to find good points in young people and help them boost their strengths. Praise their good points, and point out their weaknesses in a roundabout way, or help them to recognize their bad points on their own. These kinds of small efforts will prevent you from being disliked or shunned by young people. A small difference in the way you speak or behave will determine whether you can continuously communicate with young people. So, as you get older, it is important to be careful with the words you use and the topics you talk about, and try to build good relationships with others. Right thoughts and right words are extremely important.

### *Make resolutions every ten years to study hard And to get physically fit*

You can find many such teachings in the books of Truth I have written. I am not saying this to necessarily advertise my books, but there is more value in reading a single book by me than in reading a hundred books by others. Now, the population aged between 60 and 100 is increasing. If more and more of these people read my books, they will be able to create a future where they can stay active into their twilight years and vigorously contribute to society. This is the best way to prevent themselves from becoming a burden on younger, future generations. So, let us stay healthy and work vigorously throughout our lives.

Interestingly enough, this kind of encouragement is not always well-received outside of Japan. I heard that when our branch manager in Russia encouraged people to stay active throughout their lives, the local people got angry and said, "Are you saying that we must keep working even past 60? We should be able to retire then. How dare you teach that?" This may be because their life expectancy is shorter—around 65 or 66—due to the cold climate.*

In countries where the average life expectancy is 80 or nearly 90, people should not stop working at 60. If you make a new resolution every 10 years or so, for example, at the ages of 40, 50 and 60 to improve your knowledge and physical fitness, you will be guaranteed success in the next 10 years. Please keep this in mind and try to put in some effort. In my books, you will find many teachings like this, so I recommend you study them.

I want to say that the time has now come for the people of Japan and the world to awaken. It is time to begin anew and rise up. In order to create a bright future, we must correct our own minds and, at the same time, work together with others to play a part in creating a new society. This is important. From now on, let us take concrete actions and continue making efforts every day.

---

* According to a research in 2013, the average life expectancy in Russia is 66 years for men and 76 years for women. On the other hand, the average life expectancy in Japan is, as of 2015, 81 years for men and 87 years for women.

# AS LONG AS YOU HAVE FAITH AS THIN AS A SPIDER'S THREAD

*In times of hardship,*
*People suffer,*
*Wear out,*
*And become exhausted.*
*They speak only negative words*
*And lose the courage to believe in another day.*

*However,*
*I shall tell you.*
*As long as you have faith*
*As thin as a spider's web,*
*Buddha and God can easily save you.*

*First, believe.*
*Then, relax.*
*Buddha and God will surely provide*
*An answer to your problem.*

*Have a bright and positive mind,*
*Believing that Buddha and God will save you.*
*Be thankful*
*For what you have already been given.*
*From now on,*
*Do not overwork yourself.*
*Rather, deliberately and steadily*
*Do what you can do.*

*Believe that there is no hardship*
*Before those with an unshakable faith.*

From *A Guide for the Mind II*
*~The Way as Master and Disciple~*

# Chapter FOUR

# The Power of Miracles To Change the Era

*Religion and Politics that Can
Overcome the Era of Crisis*

# 1

# Happy Science is Expanding its Activities into Various Fields

### *We are almost complete with The first stage of development*

This chapter is the transcript of the lecture I gave in Kyushu, the southern part of Japan, in March 2016. It had been a long time since I gave a large lecture in Kyushu, but it did not mean that I was losing my love for it.

In the meantime, I was busy with various activities, including building our head temples, shoshinkans [spiritual training centers], and local branches worldwide, as well as establishing the Happy Science Academy Junior and Senior High Schools in Nasu and Kansai [western part of Japan], and the Happy Science University [HSU]. Moreover, we formed the Happiness Realization Party [HRP] and carried out various political activities. Due to these activities, I gave lectures a little less frequently. But my feelings have not changed at all since founding Happy Science.

Happy Science is an organization that grew mainly through the passionate missionary work in the Kyushu area from our early days. It was from Okinawa that missionary work through books started, and it was from this area of Kyushu that one-on-one missionary work powerfully started, preceding other areas of Japan. The Kyushu area has always been a source of inner support for me. Looking over the history of Japan, too, new things have generally started in the western region first.

Happy Science has continued its religious activities for 30 years now, and it has been 35 years since I attained Great Enlightenment. The first generation has aged and I have found that many people of my generation have retreated from the frontlines. I, however, cannot retire yet. I feel that we are almost complete with the first stage of development.

Looking back, the act of holding lectures nationwide was actually not too difficult. But expanding our organization as a religion required land, buildings, and staff. It took time to cultivate our staff, and we needed a lot of time to consider matters such as our educational and political ideals, as well as our global development. Thirty years have flown by while we worked on various activities. Now, I am astonished at the sudden passing of time. I, myself, do not feel like I am getting older, but people I have known for a long time are growing older and older. It is truly a strange feeling.

By the way, my dreams are usually about my late teens and 20s. I rarely have a dream of myself being older than 30. This could be because I got so busy and deeply absorbed in my work after I started Happy Science at the age of 30. I always keep in mind how it feels to be a young adult. I am always keenly aware of just how far I am from completing my work.

## *I want everyone to receive my messages, and for those Who can to take action*

Seven years have passed since we established Happiness Realization Party (HRP) [as of 2016]. No other activity of Happy Science has taken as long to achieve results. I am slightly surprised by this, too. Our activities span a broad range; that is why it has been so difficult. Apparently, it is true that the human head can only think of one thing at a time. You can start several things at once, but you might not be able to complete any of them unless you tackle them individually, one by one.

However, my head is not like that. You could say I am like a multi-plug socket that can hold many different power cords. Thanks to that, fortunately, my thoughts extend to various regions across the globe. Nonetheless, those who receive my messages can only make progress by doing one thing at a time.

On January 30, 2016, I gave a lecture in Okinawa entitled, "Shinjitsu no Sekai" [literally, "The World of Truth"] at the Okinawa Convention Center. [The lecture is compiled as Chapter 2 of *Gendai no Seigi-ron* (literally, "Modern Justice Theory") (Tokyo: IRH Press, 2016).] The day before the lecture, my son, Yuta Okawa, who serves as the Managing Director of Happy Science, spoke with a local temple manager in Okinawa who was also slated to be the HRP candidate for Okinawa. He told my son that he could not fully devote himself to political activities because his local temple had yet to reach its goal of happiness planting [offerings].

When I heard that I replied, "Yes, I could see that would be hard," and was keenly reminded of the difficulty in managing projects. His local temple covered a small area and it was hard for him to achieve the goal amount. So, he primarily worked on accomplishing that goal, and engaged in political activity if he had any remaining time. Hearing this, I understood very well the reason why it is taking so much time for HRP to see success. The truth of the matter is, no more than one project can be done concurrently.

But in fact, Happy Science is now involved in at least five different activities. So, when regional directors and temple managers act as the intermediary means of communication, the content of our activities is not really being transmitted very well to all our believers. Therefore, I want each and every believer to receive the messages that I am giving out, and I want those who can, to start taking action. Political activity is one of the actions. My political opinions have not changed much from the beginning.

There were many Diet members belonging to other political parties who were Happy Science devotees, back when we did not have a political party yet. Actually, there are still people like this now, and they are probably a little hesitant, waiting to see what will happen. But they do not have to hold back so much. Differences in political leanings do not mean anything to me. If you want to become a believer, by all means, please join us. I am not so narrow-minded to care about such differences.

We are simply voicing our opinions for Japan and the world to head in the direction of a better future. Each political party absorbs this information at a level that it is capable of absorbing, but Happy Science is by no means exclusive; we do not reject other religious groups. We have some understanding toward other organizations and people whose conduct is different from ours. With that understanding, we give out information about what we think is better. We do not carry out something like heresy inquisitions. People are free to join us or leave us. This is one expression of our confidence.

# 2

# Proof of the Other World is Being Provided in Real Time

✧   ✧   ✧

## *Do not let go of your faith so easily*

In the audience of the lecture on which this chapter is based, I heard there were many members that attended after being inactive for a long time. These people may have studied the Truth enough that they could find their temple managers' messages a little lacking. But they need to know that our temple managers, too, are still in the process of undergoing spiritual training. Those temple managers started studying the Truth at about the same time as other regular members, so they have yet to accumulate wisdom.

In fact, once you possess faith, you should not let it go easily. Figuratively speaking, losing your faith is like losing all the savings that you have worked so hard to accumulate. It is like having your post-retirement pension completely disappear. Moreover, discarding your faith will not only cause you to lose post-retirement security, but also to completely lose your security after death. Having your retirement money vanish into thin air will lead to hard times in your later years. But losing your faith will lead to hard times in your later years and beyond. In fact, you will have quite a difficult time after you die.

For 30 years, I have consistently preached that humans have eternal life. When you return to the other world, you will be categorized according to the kind of person you are. At that time, the first question you will be asked is, "What religion do you believe in?"

People who were atheists or materialists will automatically fail at that point. They will then be placed in an underground school where the sun never shines, and will not be able to come up to the surface until they have sufficient knowledge and understanding of the Truth. In fact, they cannot go into the sunlight because it would make them feel as if their skin was peeling off, so they would first need to study in the dark.

On the other hand, people who believed in God or Buddha will be classified according to the belief they had. Christians will be guided to a Christian group and Buddhists to a Buddhist group. There are many other groups, too, including Muslim, Jewish, Hindu, or Japanese Shinto. They will be asked, "What did you believe in the most?" or "What has the closest connection to your soul?" and will be classified based on that answer, and then an orientation course to the Spirit World would begin.

Once classified, angels will come to guide you. Or, if not angels, a spirit may come to guide you in the form of a Buddhist monk or Shinto priest. In this way, your residence in the other world will be determined, and so will the curriculum of your education and direction of your work.

In an effort to prove this truth, Happy Science has been carrying out its activities for 30 years. For example, we have conducted over 600 sessions of various readings and spiritual messages, and have published over 400 books in a series of spiritual messages, which were recorded in an open-session format [as of November 2016]. There has been no case of such level of activity anywhere else in the entire world. There has been nothing like this in history. This is being conducted in real time.

Certainly, many people throughout history have said that the other world exists. However, we also have to admit that only a few have actually set about proving the existence of the other world or proving that humans are spiritual beings. Each and every book in our spiritual message series is a step in the direction toward that proof.

This is the very reason that Happy Science boldly uses the word "science" in its name. In other words, we take the stance to thoroughly verify things and try to gather proof. People have received education in a mistaken value system and devoted themselves to work in errant ways of thinking. In this modern age when religion is fading from people's minds, we are trying to teach people their true mission.

## *All kinds of opportunities for life training Await you in this world*

It is not easy to be born into this world. You live your life in this world for some decades, then return to the other world and undertake a new lifestyle before being reborn in this world again after decades or even hundreds of years. When you do, you will have to stay in your mother's womb for several months, in a pure darkness that only allows you to slightly hear the muffled voices of people talking until you are finally born into the world in a completely powerless state.

These conditions apply to all people, no matter how great a figure they were in their past lives. Everyone is born into his or her present life crying, with the uncertainty of what will happen in his or her life. This is the pain of being born, one of the Four Pains—birth, aging, illness, and death—as taught in Buddhism.

After that, we experience all sorts of events in the tumultuous waves of life. For example, you may suffer from bullying at school. Perhaps you might be one of the bullies. You may be involved in an accident or suffer an illness. Or, you may see people close to you die, such as your parents, siblings, grandparents, or friends.

Furthermore, the home that you considered safe to be born into may face bankruptcy. Before you were born, you could have had the plan to get the highest level of education, but the circumstances of your household could change when you are actually born into this world. You may unfortunately be unable to pursue an education at the level you wanted. There may be areas of study that are brand new to you in this lifetime, so you may be unable to master them. Regarding careers as well, you may not be able to do the kind of work you wanted. You may even have to hop from job to job.

In this way, there are various life training opportunities awaiting you in this present life. This is what I meant when I said in the early days of Happy Science, "Life is like a workbook of problems to be solved." Up until our membership swelled to around 10,000 people, I often used to say that, although I would love to give you an answer, you must solve the problem you are facing by yourself. This is what we call "soul training based on self-power."

## *Numerous miracles have occurred due to outside power*

As Happy Science has expanded, however, it was not sufficient to just emphasize the soul training of each individual. We also had to include the element of saving people. In other words, we had to start including the teachings from an outside power.

Then, all sorts of miracles that we had never even imagined started happening. For example, in recent years we have seen all sorts of illnesses cured. In reality, we have actually seen things like tumors the size of a fist disappearing, people who could not stand being able to stand, and blind people gaining sight. We are also seeing things like family members who had not been getting along,

suddenly opening up to each other and regaining their old relationships. Furthermore, there are cases of people who had been
experiencing stagnation in their businesses achieving breakthroughs.

In these ways, we are seeing that coming into contact with
Happy Science teachings, connecting with Dharma friends [other
Happy Science members], or participating in our activities brings
change in people's lives. Of course, if you think about it calmly and
objectively, you can see the reason for this. A huge group of guiding
spirits is guiding us from the heavenly world.

## *Happy Science is a religion*
## *That started with tolerance as its base*

When a religion guides its people, it is extremely rare for it to reveal
the identity and name of who is actually giving guidance spiritually.
In general, when the name of the guiding spirit is given, in most cases
it is only a symbolic name. Another case is that a single divine being
gives teachings under a specific title, thereby preventing unnecessary
confusion and keeping the uniformity of the teachings. This is the
common style of religion. This is why people in general assume that
when a religion becomes the driving force behind a nation, it will try
to unify everyone's sense of values, push its ideology on people, and
lead them toward totalitarianism.

Happy Science, however, makes clear that a group of higher
guiding spirits, 500 of them, gives diverse teachings. Therefore, each
believer needs to decide for him or herself which of these teachings

to put into practice, or which teaching applies to him or her. This being so, it can sometimes seem hard for Happy Science as a whole to move forward in one direction.

But the fact that Happy Science receives different kinds of spiritual messages and inspiration from several hundred guiding spirits who had been involved in religion, politics and economy of Japan and other countries shows that Happy Science has been accepting diversity since its very beginning. In other words, it means that Happy Science is a religion that started with tolerance toward others as its base.

Thus, I am not pressuring people by saying, "My own personal ideology, creed, and ways of thinking are the only important ones, and all other ways of thinking are unacceptable." Instead, I am showing the different ways of thinking of the heavenly spirits, and suggesting the better direction to choose after revealing them. Moreover, I am also suggesting that you select ideas that correspond to the developmental stage of your mind, or those that correspond to your soul training, to proceed on your spiritual journey.

# 3

# Warnings of Crisis are
# Coming Down from Gods

✧　　✧　　✧

### *There are times when I must give
### People a crisis warning*

Happy Science has grown large as a religious organization in these
30 years. Some people describe our group as a large religious order,
while others say it may in truth be smaller than it actually appears.
Both opinions exist. Obviously, it is difficult to objectively estimate
the size of a religion. However, its number of staff members is one
objective and accurate measurement. Among all of the religious
groups in Japan, Happy Science has the second largest number of
staff members. I believe that fairly indicates the size of the religious
order. If you look at the number of staff members, you get an
overall sense of its size. We can now say that we have come so far
at this point.

In terms of the power to provide an informational voice and
express opinions, we are actually number one in Japan. There are
no other religious groups that are as up-to-date, that have this
level of modernity, that delve as much into current affairs, and that
continually speak what they think is right in the face of mistaken

journalism. In that sense, I am happy that we have become a strong religion that can stand firm and fight with our lives at stake.

At times, when I express strong opinions, I am well aware that some people have difficulty following us. Of course, as I stated earlier, our basic stance is to welcome as many people to join us with a spirit of tolerance, and I do have the wish that they can follow our beliefs. Nevertheless, each time that I sense a crisis coming, I give a strong warning that people must change their direction due to the potential danger. At those times, people who are unable to understand what I say probably distance themselves a bit from Happy Science for some time. Perhaps it is fine to have such periods.

However, the truth of the matter is this. At the end of the day, there is a substantial difference between the knowledge and intelligence of humans on earth, and the thoughts of gods and high spirits close to gods in the higher realms of the Spirit World far above the earthly world. The reason is that they can see much more than human beings can.

There are times when crisis warnings come to us, and there are times when we receive forecasts of prosperity. I sometimes speak about various matters much earlier than other people do. These messages include good as well as bad ones. Sometimes I wish I could just talk about good forecasts only, but there are also times when I must speak out about an impending crisis.

Recently, for example, numerous special features on the Great East Japan Earthquake of March 11, 2011, appeared on television and in newspapers. A few months before that earthquake occurred,

I warned people through the spiritual messages of Amaterasu-O-Mikami [the Sun Goddess] that a massive disaster would hit Japan [see, *Saidai Kofuku Shakai no Jitsugen ~Amaterasu-O-Mikami no Kinkyu Shinji~* (literally, "The Realization of a Society of the Greatest Happiness ~An Urgent Divine Revelation from Amaterasu-O-Mikami~") (Tokyo: IRH Press, 2010)]. It came about exactly as I had warned. I had also already spoken on the cause of the disaster.

However, not knowing these messages, not just a few people only interpret the physical phenomenon and try to pull people even further from the hearts of the gods. This is truly sad.

## I have been calling attention to a national crisis since The launch of our political party

In recent years, I have also been calling attention to a national crisis since we founded the Happiness Realization Party in 2009. Honestly speaking, this is a painful task as a religious leader. There have been many times when I truly wish that politicians did their jobs properly, so that I do not need to say any of these things.

Other religious groups just insist on absolute peace. They most likely have no understanding about what is going on in the world, even if they read the newspaper or watch television. I am incredibly envious because if you do not know anything, you can live happily in a bubble, just insisting on absolute peace.

Perhaps they could care less about what is happening in the world. They seem to be totally caught up in their own personal lives, completely believing that Japan is safe as long as it continuously adheres to one-country pacifism. There would be no problem if nothing bad actually happens; all they have to be concerned about is the missing social security money they are supposed to receive when they get older.

However, it is extremely clear to me that problems will certainly occur, and that is why I am speaking out about our national crisis. For example, in 2009 when we founded the Happiness Realization Party, North Korea launched a missile. The Liberal Democratic Party of Japan was in power at that time, and Taro Aso was the prime minister. Japan simply observed the event and had absolutely no ability to respond.

One year earlier, in 2008, there was the incident in which the Chief of Staff of Japan Air Self-Defense Force, Toshio Tamogami, was fired just for writing an essay about how Japan was not an aggressor nation. This is indicative of the flawed stance that the Liberal Democratic Party of Japan took in the face of an imminent crisis.

After that, the Democratic Party of Japan came into power and the policy began to take a 180-degree turn. The first DPJ Prime Minister Yukio Hatoyama said things like, "I want to make the waters of Asia a sea of friendship." However, right now, in this "sea of friendship" is an island that China built by filling in a coral reef, from which fighter jets can be launched. In addition, there are an island with an approximately two-mile runway and an island equipped with surface-to-air missiles. It is not just recently that China started to take these islands. Since the 1970s, China started to claim remote islands that were subjects of territorial disputes with places like Taiwan, the Philippines, Vietnam, and Malaysia, little by little. And those activities still continue today.

China has even boldly surrounded an American aircraft carrier when it passed through the South China Sea as part of the Freedom of Navigation Program.* This is a horrific situation. Things that someone in the 20th century could never have imagined are happening now. In other words, simply spouting the rhetoric of "absolute peace" does not necessarily lead to these problems going away. This is the current climate in Asia.

## *China is planning to unilaterally dominate Asia*

I have also warned several times about the problem of North Korea. North Korea has already conducted four nuclear weapon tests. [At the time of the lecture. On September 9, 2016, North Korea conducted the fifth test.] The fourth test, conducted on January 6, 2016, was particularly notable in that it was a hydrogen bomb test. The international community is reluctant to admit this, but Kim Jong-un himself has made that claim. He also said they have succeeded in miniaturizing nuclear weaponry and have started to test short-range missiles, firing them into areas near Japan. Later in the year, the U.S.

---

* The United States of America deploys U.S. warships and aircraft to international waters and airspace to monitor the free navigation of the high seas and skies. On April 4, 2016, the U.S. Department of Defense revealed that USS John C. Stennis found a multitude of Chinese warships surrounding it in the South China Sea during its surveillance operation.

and South Korea began joint military training operations on a massive scale unequalled in the past, and executed ocean-to-land landing exercises. It was during this training operation that North Korea test fired a missile from a submarine.

We recorded a spiritual message from the guardian spirit of Kim Jong-un and urgently published it in January 2016 [see, *Kita-Chosen Kim Jong-un ha Naze Suibaku Jikken o Shita-noka* (literally, "Why Did North Korean Kim Jong-un Conduct Hydrogen Bomb Testing?") (Tokyo: IRH Press, 2016)]. In it, the guardian spirit of Kim Jong-un said something along the lines of, "Even if the U.S. attacks us, actually, North Korea is linked with Iran. We are exporting missile technology to them, so our missiles can also launch from Iran." In fact, after the U.S. started military exercises, a ballistic missile was launched from Iran too, and the U.S. is petitioning the UN for sanctions. In his spiritual message, the guardian spirit of Kim Jong-un predicted that North Korea and Iran would share an underground linkage, and that even the U.S. would not be able to attack two places simultaneously. This was what exactly happened.

To delve even further into this, some of the ballistic missile technology used by North Korea and Iran actually come from China. Thus, while China puts on a pretense of imposing sanctions on North Korea, we can see that this is not their true stance. If they wanted to stop exporting to North Korea, they could stop all variety of items including petroleum, but they will never do that. The reason for this is that China is letting North Korea act recklessly in their stead. Therefore, I must say that although nations like the U.S.,

Europe, and Japan think they need the help of China to suppress North Korea, they do not really know what China is thinking.

Unfortunately, in the world, politics and diplomacy are not conducted based solely on honesty. The truth is that many people have underlying motivations and are trying to push things in the direction that will most benefit them. China is now clearly trending toward unilateral domination of Asia, and this will probably rise to the surface more clearly when China surpasses the American economy.

On the other hand, sadly, the U.S. is showing more and more signs of its decline. Decline is gradually but surely setting in, just as how the tide recedes. Though it was previously thought that the era of global supremacy for the U.S. as a superpower would last a century, as soon as the door of the 21st century opened, China immediately stepped onto the stage as a major rival. What's more, China is already putting together a vision for what they will do after they surpass the United States. But no one has yet to prescribe any countermeasure against it. Right now, no one has been able to offer any ideas.

# 4

# The Ideal State of Japanese Politics

### *The post-war pro-constitution stance*
### *Is approaching a turning point*

With these kinds of changes as a backdrop, Japan must consider the issue of its constitution. In Japan, a new constitution was drafted after its defeat in WWII, and people were forced to maintain the pro-constitutional stance even in the educational system and the political arena. We have been taught for years that compliance was the basis for peace.

However, I now strongly feel that a turning point is approaching concerning the circumstances of this long-held stance. To put it plainly, although the preamble to the Constitution of Japan states, "(...) we have determined to preserve our security and existence, trusting in the justice and faith of the peace-loving peoples of the world," countries surrounding Japan currently include people other than just "peace-loving people."

Obviously, every country has its own unique ideology and way of thinking. The concepts of freedom, democracy, a parliamentary system, and rule-of-law proposed by the U.S. and Europe are not necessarily regarded highly all the time. In fact, if you listen to the true feelings of China, you will hear that they have never experienced success under any system other than an authoritarian government. In China, there has only been national stability when the government completely purges all opposition and succeeds in autocratic domination. In times without this domination, the country experienced many eras of division and internal fighting. For this reason, they probably feel deeply in their hearts that they can never trust any democratic government. They most probably think that the human rights diplomacy the U.S. advocates is completely absurd, and that if you give sovereignty to the people, the country will instantly be overthrown. Therefore, it is a matter of course that the U.S. and China cannot be on the same page.

For example, in the late 90s during the Clinton administration in the U.S., the following event happened: When the U.S. decided to apply sanctions on China due to its persecution of human rights activists, China pretended to ease up right away. However, once the U.S. gave China most favored nation status and showered it with preferential economic treatment, China immediately turned around and arrested several hundred anti-government activists. This is the true character of China.

As this example shows, they have their own values in which they firmly believe, and they do not easily change. Also, looking at things historically, you cannot say with absolute confidence which view is correct. Nevertheless, we now appreciate things like freedom, equality, and democracy, or parliamentary democracy, and rule-of-law—systems that allow people with different values to discuss matters and decide their future direction. We consider these values as beneficial and adopt them. So, when some nations try to do away with those values, unfortunately, we cannot work with them because we are in a position to work hard to spread those values.

## *Easily misunderstood viewpoints In current Japanese politics*

Looking at the current state of politics in Japan, some issues can easily be misunderstood. First is the issue of Taiwan. Recently I published a book, *Kinkyu Shugorei Interview: Taiwan Shin-Soto Tsai Ing-wen no Mirai Senryaku* [literally, "Urgent Guardian Spirit Interview: The Future Strategy of New Taiwanese President Tsai Ing-wen" (Tokyo: IRH Press, 2016)]. I am afraid to say that Japan is ignorant of the geo-political significance of Taiwan. This goes for not only the people of Japan, but also its politicians and the mass media.

Right now, Hong Kong is under the thumb of the Beijing government. If Taiwan were to be absorbed into mainland China, they would follow the same path as Hong Kong. Should that happen, Japan would not be able to import a single drop of oil from the Arabian Peninsula. In other words, Japan would not be able to produce energy through fossil fuels. Japanese people have to get a much clearer understanding on this.

Despite being in such a situation, the nuclear power plant accident that occurred during the 2011 Great East Japan Earthquake sparked a movement to completely eliminate nuclear power plants within 20 to 30 years. This movement has spread for the past five years as though it is the correct stance. Left-wingers and environmentalists have come together, saying that this would be the right decision that best accords with justice. Honestly speaking, the underlying thoughts come from the Chinese government.

However, what would happen to Japan if its nuclear power plants were shut down and its petroleum imports were completely blocked? Furthermore, what would happen if Japan were to come under the threat of nuclear weapons when in fact it cannot arm itself with these? This would signify that China could take Japan without a fight.

Alternatively, instead of China, North Korea could take over Japan. If Japan's diplomatic relations with the U.S. grow much worse to the point that the U.S. would no longer help Japan in times of a crisis, then even a small nation with only 20 million people like North Korea could possibly take Japan. North Korea may be a small nation, but it has over 1.1 million soldiers. On the other hand, Japan has about 230,000 JSDF [Japan Self-Defense Forces] troops. Furthermore, they have more naval ships than Japan, with about 780 in total. They also have numerous missiles.

We do not know if North Korea has truly succeeded in miniaturizing nuclear warheads until they actually shoot one, but if they do launch one, it might be too late to do anything about it. Suppose North Korea has nuclear weapons that can precisely hit their targets when fired. What would the Japanese government do? In that case, unless the U.S. displays the resolve to sacrifice the lives of American soldiers unconditionally for Japan, the lifeline of Japan will rest firmly within the grip of those countries' powers.

## *Politicians should be honest to their citizens*
## *And to foreign countries*

As a religious leader, I cannot put the entire Japanese population in danger. I am not saying this as a political claim only. For me, it does not matter which party takes how many seats in the Diet. I have no interest in something like that. In truth, I am fine with any party. But since there are no risk-taking parties in Japan now, Happy Science has set foot into the political arena. We can do this because we have the physical and mental strength to continue asserting our opinions even while receiving criticisms that come from the domestic and conventional post-war view of history, which has been going on for 70 years.

However, other political parties in Japan are different. As soon as they are criticized, they change their assertions and nonchalantly adopt the completely opposite opinion. When they are elected, they do things that are completely different from what they had said when they were campaigning. I want this kind of politics to stop. Politicians should be honest to their people and to foreign countries as well. I believe major powers have a responsibility to continuously lead the people of the world in the right direction.

Some of our members belong to the Liberal Democratic Party of Japan [LDP], so I feel bad for repeatedly criticizing Prime Minister Abe. Nonetheless, regarding the relocation of a U.S. military base on Okinawa, although an effort was being made to solve the problem by moving it to the Henoko area within Okinawa, Prime

Minister Abe suspended the work after being suggested by the court to compromise.*

One source says that Prime Minister Abe has become obsessed about relocating the U.S. Marine Corps to a remote island near Tanegashima Island in Kagoshima Prefecture,† and has already brought up the idea to the U.S. forces. If he suddenly makes an official announcement on this, the Okinawan media will rejoice, the people of Okinawa Prefecture will rejoice, the left wing camp in Japan will rejoice, and he may win the next election by a landslide. However, it is wrong to make decisions about these kinds of national defense or diplomacy policies based solely on election strategy. He must consider the real issues at hand.

## *Japan should not allow Okinawa to be taken With a single statement*

On the other hand, China is claiming that Okinawa and the Senkaku Islands are Chinese territory and their core interests. Usually, you won't be able to say something like this. What if Japan made

---

* The central government filed a lawsuit to seek administrative subrogation action against the Okinawa Prefectural Governor Takeshi Onaga over the cancellation of the landfill approval to build a replacement facility for the Marine Corps Air Station Futenma in the Henoko district in Nago City. The Fukuoka High Court accepted the lawsuit in September 2016. Previously, on March 4, 2016, the central government and the prefectural government both accepted the court-mediated settlement proposed by the Fukuoka High Court and decided to suspend the ongoing construction project.

† On the issue of the relocation of the Futenma U.S. base, Keitaro Hasegawa, a leading Japanese international economist, revealed that Prime Minister Abe is considering relocating the base to a place outside of Okinawa, to Mageshima Island in the East China Sea, about seven miles west of Tanegashima, Kagoshima.

a similar claim? For example, Japan could claim the Liaodong Peninsula as Japanese territory because Japan took it after winning the First Sino-Japanese War. Or, it could take the Kuril Islands just by stating that they are also Japanese territory. How easy would it be to take territory just by saying it belongs to us. In reality, however, this is not something one could ever say. Neither the Japanese prime minister nor any government spokesperson would actually be able to make such a claim. Yet, China is actually doing this.

Furthermore, China is building more and more military base facilities on the Spratly Islands, the Paracel Islands, and on surrounding areas. They are building military bases in areas where they claim territorial rights. They are just taking unilateral action with such behavior; this is the true nature of a dictatorship. In other words, there is no opposition in their country. Those who oppose would be purged and their entire family would disappear, so no one is able to oppose. China makes it seem as if they operate through the NPC [National People's Congress], which is supposed to be like a parliamentary body, but it is just a formality. So, there is no one who can actually mount an opposition. This kind of frightening aspect exists; we should be well aware of it.

Japan should not allow Okinawa to be taken with a single statement. I love the people of Okinawa, so if in compromise the government puts forth the proposal to relocate the U.S. Marine Corps to a remote island in Kagoshima Prefecture, I would have to warn them to stop and think twice because it would undoubtedly lead to Okinawa being taken. Okinawa would definitely be taken because the U.S. would hardly risk their soldiers' lives to fight and protect people who do not appreciate them. This is not how diplomacy should be; we cannot fight unless we unite as one.

If Donald Trump from the Republican Party becomes the next American president, he will most likely demand Japan to develop an appropriate power of self-defense. If Hillary Clinton of the Democratic Party becomes the president, she will pay lip service saying that she will protect Japan, but will choose a path not to fight China in an actual war because she will want to protect the economic benefits that come from China. The truth of the matter is that the nation with the stronger desire would actualize those desires in the end.

# 5

# Japan Needs to Wake Up

✧ ✧ ✧

### *Religious spirit has been lost in post-war Japan*

I believe that the Japanese people have lived in a good and peaceful era for over 70 years since the end of WWII and have developed economically as well. Unfortunately, however, Japan has lost its religious spirit during that time.

Recently, dark books such as *Jiin Shometsu* [literally, "Vanishing Temples"] and *Shukyo Shometsu* [literally, "Vanishing Religion"] have been published in Japan. It is indeed true that religion is on the wane. All sorts of religious groups are on the verge of disappearing, with the number of temples and the people who run them decreasing.

Simply put, faith is diminishing. Rather, the number of people who do not believe in the other world, God, nor Buddha is rising. There are plenty of people who think that life is limited to this world, who are only concerned with protecting their lives on earth, and who think they are happy as long as they can be healed of illnesses, have plenty to eat and have a place to live.

The Japanese mass media have frequently used the phrase, "a prayer to console the departed souls" regarding the near 20,000 people who lost their lives in the Great East Japan Earthquake. But do they really understand the true meaning of those words? To truly understand the phrase, "a prayer to console the departed souls," you need to understand the existence of the soul and the spirit, the existence of God and Buddha, and the existence of the Spirit World.

Happy Science affirms the existence of the other world and gives opinions based on this premise. We are not promoting war by saying that life on earth is not valuable. It is quite the opposite. We state that the way one lives in this world determines the way one will live in the other world. Based on this truth, I hope the lives of many people to shine honorably. I do not want individuals to simply serve for others' gain. Rather, I hope each person aims to live his or her own life to the fullest, making that life shine righteously. I believe that is the best part of democracy.

## *A divine-nature, or Buddha-nature, Resides within everyone*

From the standpoint of God or Buddha, the idea that humans have sovereignty could well be an extremely arrogant way of thinking. But the Buddhist philosophy teaches that every person has Buddha-nature within. By this, Shakyamuni Buddha meant that everyone has the potential to attain enlightenment, not that everyone is already a buddha. He taught, "If you accumulate spiritual training, purify your heart, and pray for other people's happiness, you can enter the path to becoming a buddha. All types of people have their own path to become a bodhisattva or a buddha."

Christianity, on the other hand, teaches that Jesus is the only son of God, but that way of thinking is mistaken. It is indeed true that Jesus was a great historical figure and a spiritual leader sent by God, but there are many others who can feel and convey the words of God, or who can manifest profound faith for the sake of God.

I believe that divine-nature and Buddha-nature resides in every single person. I also think that more and more people need to find faith, and make efforts for the sake of humanity and for the love of their neighbors, instead of solely seeking their own benefit. Religion is an extremely important organization to teach this and enlighten people. Thus, we cannot accept the post-war climate that belittles religion.

Furthermore, Happy Science thoroughly and squarely challenges the materialistic philosophy stating that religions are not necessary because many wars are caused by religious conflict. The truth is that the cause does not lie in religion. Conflict among humans does not end because the teachings of God are not being passed down accurately.

## Fulfill the mission given to Happy Science

Right now, Happy Science is the one and only Japanese religion with the potential to become a world religion. As a newly emerging religion, I believe we must voice our opinions from Japan to the world. If we do not do this right now, who will?

I am not saying that I have resentment for China or North Korea. They are extremely important, in a historical sense as well.

I want to bring freedom to them also. I want to give them the dignity all humans deserve. I want them to awaken to their Buddha-nature or divine nature. And I want them to join us in creating a Buddhaland utopia. That is why we must crack through their shell of mistaken values with all our might since they are firmly set on their values. This is the mission of Happy Science.

Happy Science is also involved in political activities. We are not doing this for our own profit. Some of our candidates have lost up to six or seven elections, and that is an extremely painful experience. Imagine how horrible it would be to fail an exam that many times. Still, they keep going. Why? The answer is, they are not doing it for their own benefit. Someone has to tackle this. We are engaging in political activities because we know that someone has to overcome the commonly held beliefs we have lived with since the end of WWII. Someone has to speak out about our national crisis.

Thus, this is not the time for our believers to stay inactive. If we do not stand up right now, it will be too late. If we do not spread this philosophy throughout Japan and throughout the world now, it will be too late. This is the final warning. It might really be the last chance before everything is over.

Sakurajima erupted, as did Mount Aso, both in Kyushu, southern Japan. Think hard on what this means and about what is waiting for us in the future. The Great East Japan Earthquake did not occur to make the people of Japan suffer. Warnings are coming down from Heaven, telling Japan to wake up.

In foreign countries, on the other hand, some people are trying to control other countries with fear. However, you cannot force people to follow you through fear. Only love will inspire people to follow. And only love can change the world.

This is why Happy Science was created. I have been active for some 30 years now, and I will not stop until I die. Please follow me until the very end.

The one standing before you is El Cantare, the Lord of all gods. Please do not forget this fact.

Chapter FIVE

# Awakening to the Power of Mercy

*May Love Reach the Hearts of Many*

# *1*

# The Ultimate Solution
# To End Religious Wars

✧　　✧　　✧

## *Before preaching on the theme of mercy*

Mercy is a theme I have sometimes spoken on in foreign countries [on September 18, 2011, Ryuho Okawa gave a lecture entitled, "The Age of Mercy" in Malaysia], but I have not spoken on it much in Japan. Thinking about why this was the case, I feel it was because Happy Science has valued the spirit of self-help from the very beginning. Talks on mercy would mainly be addressed to those in need of being saved, so I did not want Happy Science to start at such a position.

Recently, however, as seen from examples like the Great East Japan Earthquake, tragic events are continuously occurring unabated in various places throughout the Japanese Archipelago. In fact, after the Great East Japan Earthquake, I received several letters from Happy Science members saying things like, "In the wake of such an earthquake disaster, it would be very reassuring to have a large prayer hall in the Sendai area. Could you please build one?"

After reading these letters, I immediately decided to erect Sendai Shoshinkan. Though it would not be completed soon enough to provide concrete aid, I built a slightly large temple, hoping it would serve as a lighthouse to guide people's hearts [Sendai Shoshinkan opened in July 2012]. How much salvation this has actually provided is still unknown but, as was made clear with the words "Good News" that came to me when I attained Great Enlightenment, I believe that the laws I teach must be a gospel to the people of Japan and the world.

Thirty years have passed since I gave a lecture to a little less than 90 people at the First Turning of the Dharma Wheel in November 1986 [on November 23, 1986, Ryuho Okawa gave his very first lecture, "For the Launching of Happy Science" at the Happy Science Launch Commemoration Session]. At that time, it was a very small beginning, and I may not have really been able to foresee how much power the continuous turning of the Dharma Wheel would come to have. But I am now thankful for the fact that by the time the Great East Japan Earthquake occurred, Happy Science had grown powerful enough to be able to build Sendai Shoshinkan when it was needed.

## The continuous fighting between Christianity and Islam for over a thousand years

Having said that, however, as I look at each part of Japan and various incidents happening around the world, I still feel that our influence has yet to spread far enough. The power of mercy, which is the theme of this chapter, is the fundamental light that comes from God and Buddha, and many religions speak of it. And yet, many bloody acts of terrorism and war involving religions break out. This fills me with a great deal of sadness.

Right now Europe, especially France, is outraged by the attacks from extremists in the Islamic world. On the flip side, air bombings by the West on the Islamic State are gaining intensity. On seeing this, I am overwhelmed by sadness too deep for words. I have no words. I understand that both sides have their own reasons to attack, but I feel so sad to see that those with different views can hardly come to a mutual understanding.

Islam is a religion that wishes for the power of the all-merciful Allah to extend to everyone. In reality, though, the believers of Allah on earth have no idea of the actual scope of Allah's wish for salvation.

Islam fought Christianity in three of the major Crusades in the past, and the battle still goes on today, though warfare has changed a great deal recently with the use of drones. The U.S. can now launch small, unmanned aircraft operated from remote terminals and viewed on camera-fed screens to attack, for example, the Islamic State or parts of Pakistan while staying in their own country. Since it feels as if they are playing a video game, it is probably hard for them to realize that they are actually taking human life. It is extremely painful to actually see the dead bodies of people you had killed in real time, but we are now entering an era where it only feels as though you are playing a video game rather than fighting an actual battle.

On the other hand, those being attacked in this way are doing things like getting on a theater stage and randomly shooting people in the audience, attaching explosives to their bodies and blowing themselves up in a crowded place, or putting explosives in empty cans to force airplanes to crash. They try to resist desperately using such methods. Although both sides live in the same era of technology, one side uses fighting techniques that seem extremely primitive. It feels like there is a great disparity in eras here, and I feel sadness too deep for words. This is a battle with no end.

But why is there no end to this? It is because all involved have not acquired the ultimate solution.

Why have Christianity and Islam been at odds for more than a thousand years? In the late medieval period, Islam penetrated into Europe, and the Holy Roman Empire came very close to collapse. It was an era in which Christianity was in a very precarious position. In other words, it was a time when all of Europe could have been converted to Islam. After that, however, Christian nations regained power along with the rise of Protestantism and the Industrial Revolution. And if things continue to proceed as they are now, it could possibly lead to the destruction of Islamic countries.

Looking at this historical flow, we can see that we are now faced with some major questions. Will new innovations occur in the near future? Will God bestow new power? How will our civilization change?

We, Happy Science, have already provided answers to these questions. Unfortunately, however, I must say that the answers we have provided have yet to spread widely enough throughout Japan and the world. I am very sad about this point.

# 2

# The Teachings of Love to Gain Mutual Understanding

✧   ✧   ✧

## *The element present in Japanese Shinto But lacking in Islam*

During World War II or the Great East Asia War, the West probably saw Japan in the same way they are seeing the Islamic State, which they are now bombing. It is true that there are similar elements in the roots of Islam and Japanese Shinto, as was made clear in spiritual research that Happy Science conducted [see, *The Laws of Justice* (New York: IRH Press, 2016) and *Shukyo Shakaigaku Gairon* (literally, "Introduction to Religious Sociology") (Tokyo: IRH Press, 2014)]. However, there is one difference between their teachings.

What is it that is present in Japanese Shinto but lacking in Islam? It is the existence of the Sun Goddess Amaterasu-O-Mikami. It was my third son Yuta who pointed this out to me. He said to me, "When establishing a nation-state, Japan and the Islamic nations used military force to unify the nation and then established a state religion. In this regard, they implemented very similar methods. However, Japan had Amaterasu-O-Mikami, and her light of harmony created the heart of Yamato [the spirit of Japan]. This aspect is fundamentally different from the Islamic nations."

In Japan, this power of harmony served as a strength to absorb various philosophies, studies, and religions from foreign countries, preventing Japan to be shut in its own exclusive self-righteousness. In this sense, Japan is very tolerant and this generosity is a manifestation of this power of harmony. This is worthy to note.

## Problems concerning idol worship are born from The narrow-mindedness of humans

When I previously went to Sendai to give a lecture, from the window of my hotel I saw a statue of Kannon [the Buddhist goddess of mercy] that seemed to be more than 300 feet high. I thought that if a Muslim extremist were to see it, he would probably want to destroy it immediately. Since there is such a large statue in the middle of a city, some people may want to destroy it. However, they must realize that their impulse for destruction comes from a fundamental lack of understanding.

According to the teachings of Islam, idol worship is considered wrong. In ancient Judaism as well, Moses gave teachings that also held that idol worship was wrong. Honestly speaking, however, there is a slight misunderstanding on this point.

In fact, the ban of idol worship started with the idea that God is different from humans and is an incomparably great Being. If God is expressed in the form of an idol, people may mistakenly believe that this is how God truly is, and they may start to think of God and humans on equal footing. They might start to think that God is basically the same as humans. Thus, one should have faith in God without expressing Him in that sort of a form. This was the starting point of denial of idol worship.

The same idea exists in Buddhism. Buddhist statues were built in great numbers from the era of Mahayana Buddhism, but prior to that, for nearly 500 years after Shakyamuni Buddha, there were no such things as Buddha's statues. Instead, there were many representations of the Buddha without form, such as depicting the Buddha as the Dharma Wheel or by stone footprints of the Buddha. The thinking behind this was that the Buddha was too revered to be expressed through mere physical means.

Feeling awe toward powers that are not of this world is an extremely important part of religion. However, people are getting the wrong idea if they are making this too much of a formality and harboring the desire to destroy all representational objects. It is only natural that as time passes, people would want to not only imagine in their mind what they revere, but to actually see it with their own eyes and feel it.

Thus, what was not sufficiently made clear when the original teaching appeared, can be a source of future calamity, leading people to reject other religions or to eliminate from this earth anything that is different. This is extremely sad. The narrow-mindedness of human beings is what we should lament the most.

## *Accepting and understanding differences as Differences are also love*

In the teachings of Happy Science, integration of all religions is one of our major concepts; this has been our aim from the very beginning of our foundation. In my book *The Laws of the Sun* (New York: IRH Press, 2013) as well, I clearly state that Buddhism, Christianity, and other religions actually stemmed from one fundamental source.

I wrote the book *The Laws of the Sun* when I was still around 30 years old, so while passages with rich sensibility are still very vivid, the book overall has many naive parts and areas where I did not go into enough detail. When I reread it now, there are a few things about which I am a little embarrassed. Nevertheless, I did express my desire to create a new utopian society on earth. I wrote, "People need to know that all religions were derived from one fundamental source and that those teachings came from that same source. This being so, rather than emphasizing differences and fighting over them, we should know, understand, and trust each other more. In this way, we can create a utopia." This feeling was apparent from the outset, when I published my early theoretical books.

I am now trying to fill in these large gaps between world religions. What is more, I am also trying to unveil God's or Buddha's intentions toward all human activities, including academic studies and ways of thinking.

Recently, I also started talking about the differences between various races of the world and, furthermore, about the existence of various extraterrestrial life forms that differ from humankind on Earth. To be more accurate, I am saying that sometimes differences in people's race, religion, and culture are due to the differences of their home planets. Based on an understanding that differences exist, we are all born as contemporaries into this soul training ground called the Earth, where we try to create new lifestyle patterns, civilizations, culture, philosophies, and ways of thinking while struggling in the midst of various environments. A variety of souls come to Earth to try to establish righteous ways of thinking and to live as earthlings. They come to figure out and form righteous value systems, morals, and religion on the Earth.

This is not done to cause confusion among humanity. Instead, it is to urge people to awaken to new potential by recognizing the differences. By knowing the differences, we can realize that we still have room to change. There are indeed differences in each religion, but that should not lead people to destroy all other religions. Instead, when people find elements in other religions that do not exist in their own, they should analyze what those elements are, and work to innovate their religion to enhance its power to improve humanity.

It is not as though everything was created perfectly out of a uniform mold from the very beginning. Humans were not created all uniformly in a robot factory. People are all born with differing intentions and various goals, which is why each person has a different life goal and mission.

Accepting these differences and understanding other people are also one aspect of love. When people cannot love someone, it is because they cannot understand that person. When they come to understand the other person, they come to love him or her. Because people cannot understand each other, they hate each other; because they cannot understand, they attack. Because people cannot understand, they exclude others; because they cannot understand, the chain of hateful acts never ends.

Do not think it a matter of course that this chain of hatred never ends. We must not extend the chain of hatred. Rather, once we have realized how much we do not understand the way others think, we should move forward toward mutual understanding, even if it takes one step at a time.

# 3

# Knowing Leads to Salvation

✧　　✧　　✧

**We continue to publish our teachings in order to offer**
**A gospel to each person**

Happy Science was not created to bring confusion or chaos to this world. It was established to explain the existing differences, to help people understand each other and to live in harmony, thereby creating a great new utopia.

The year, 2016, marked the 35th anniversary since I attained Great Enlightenment, the 30th anniversary of the foundation of Happy Science, and the 25th anniversary of the legal establishment of Happy Science as a religious body. All these years, our believers have worked hard to spread the teachings. I, too, have steadily accumulated a body of work, as if laying small bricks one by one.

The lecture I gave at the Celebration of the Lord's Descent in July 2016 was entitled, "The Light that Will Save the Earth," and in it I announced that it was my 2,500th lecture. In November of the previous year, we held a publishing commemoration assembly for my 2,000th book, *The Laws of Justice.* ["Commemoration Party for Publishing Over 2,000 Books in the Ryuho Okawa Book Series" was held at the Josui Hall in Tokyo.] [As of March 2017, Ryuho Okawa has published over 2,200 books.]

I understand that 2,000 books sound like a massive number, and most people would not be able to read them all. I did not write 2,000 books intending to cram all the contents into every reader's head. I have published this many books because the teachings that a person needs vary from person to person.

Some may say that I do not need to publish so many books. Others may think one book a year is more than enough. I can understand such feelings. However, that is not enough. Of course, core teachings like the Laws series are definitely necessary, but there are also many other teachings that complement those, as well as teachings that each person might currently need, even if such teachings are not directly related to the core teachings. That is why I keep publishing our teachings in order to offer a gospel to each person.

## The teachings of Happy Science are threads of Salvation for all kinds of people

Currently, Happy Science is entering a difficult phase in its management. The organization is growing so large that the entire group can no longer take uniform action toward a common goal.

For example, some people have joined Happy Science to find out the cause of their serious illness and to cure it, but they may be asked to join in political activities to support the Happiness Realization Party. Other Happy Science members around them may be interested in my teachings on space-people readings and may wonder which planet they came from. Happy Science is extending its activities to various fields, so some people may not be fully aware of what is going on. Thus, we may not be able to summon up and exert the full power of the entire organization.

Nevertheless, in a way it is good to have such a variety. There are many different ways of thinking and a variety of people, and within that diversity each person rows his or her small boat to search out his or her own direction to advance. If we allow for such variety, we will not become a totalitarian movement with a small, limited mindset to repel, push out, or eliminate everything that is different. This is why it is important to allow various ways of thinking.

Providing many different teachings does not mean we are

sowing seeds of confusion; rather, I hope you take it to mean that right now, threads of salvation are continuously provided toward all sorts of people. Some of my teachings may not be directly related to the people of Japan, but related to people in other countries. Some of my books may seem religious to Japanese people, but to people of other countries, those may be read as books to establish a nation or laws to stop the chain of war.

## Religious conflicts arise due to the lack of teachings

Those who study the Truth at Happy Science learn about our teachings on extraterrestrial beings as well, so when they meet someone whom they find difficult to understand, they may say to themselves, "Perhaps that person comes from another planet. There is no way we can see eye to eye if our planets of origin are not the same." They may be able to find peace of mind in that way.

Even if our original home planets were different, we are now on the same planet Earth as similar earthly beings participating in the same experiment on civilization. Despite being on the same planet Earth, if our home country or nationality is different, or if the religion or political system of our country is different, we could be brought up to assimilate ways of thinking that are different from our original ways after several decades. For this reason, some choose to be reborn into different countries. I have given many teachings on these secrets of reincarnation.

However, reincarnation is not clearly taught in the Bible, so people with Christian backgrounds sometimes reject the teachings of reincarnation and say that it is heresy, or something they should not believe in. This happens because there are missing pieces in what they have been taught.

There is no way Jesus Christ had no knowledge of the mechanism of being born into this world from the other world. Actually, it is merely that his teachings on reincarnation have not really been passed down to the current day. However, modern clerics cannot accept this concept, so when they hear the teachings of reincarnation, they quickly assume that such teachings are heretical and wrong. They compare those teachings with past religions that were eradicated through heresy trials.

Christians also think that Islam is a heretical religion. When it comes to Islam, on the other hand, when we recorded a spiritual message from Muhammad, he said that the teachings of Christianity are of the devil [see, *Spiritual Messages from Prophet Muhammad— On the Paris Shooting—Freedom of Expression vs. Faith in Islam,* (Tokyo: Happy Science, 2015)]. This is how radical they are. This could simply be regarded as differences in opinion, but if both sides were to actually take up swords and kill each other, that would lead to something horrific. Although it is fine to have different arguments, we need to create a framework that is generous enough to encompass them all.

## *Knowledge can serve as a reference When making decisions*

Currently, my books are being published in many different languages. This is a very important thing. Knowledge can serve as a reference when making decisions. You can stop and reconsider things when you are confronted with a different way of thinking. This is an extremely important process.

Happy Science translates work into 28 languages and publishes various books of Truth, all without seeking profit. Since people of countries with lower economic levels cannot really afford our books, we are actually distributing our books almost free of charge. My books contain many facts that people are exposed to for the very first time, and they are often shocked to know the Truth. This is why we need to educate people in this way.

Right now, many conflicts are occurring all around the world between those who do not understand each other. We cannot leave these conflicts to continue.

Happy Science books may naturally contain topics that do not directly relate to you. For example, some people may not find our book about the secrets of fashion interesting [see, *Fashion Sense no Migaki kata* (literally, "Tips to Improve Your Fashion Sense") (Tokyo: IRH Press, 2016)]. But it is also true that other people find salvation through that very same book.

We also publish books about healing illnesses through the power of mind [see, *Healing Power* (Tokyo: HS Press, 2016), *Byoki-Karma*

*Reading* (literally, "Readings on Illness Karma") (Tokyo: IRH Press, 2015)]. Some who work at hospitals may refuse to read those books. However, by knowing that illnesses can be created by one's mental attitude, one can gain the power to improve his or her condition. So, this is an extremely important idea. An enormous amount of tax money is being spent on elderly welfare and illness treatment. This is largely due to the influence of the current epidemic of materialist thought. Since we are heading into a highly aging society, we need to do something to decrease the number of people who would be confined to beds, waiting to be saved.

# 4

# Awaken to the Power of Mercy Dormant in You

## *The importance of knowing the meaning of death*

In the end, there is a question common to all people. This applies to everyone, regardless of who you are or your nationality. It relates to mercy, the theme of this chapter. That question is, "What is death?"

Some people live past the age of one hundred, but no matter

how hard they may try, no one can escape death. Even Konosuke Matsushita, the founder of Panasonic, who said that he was going to live to the age of 160, passed away at 94. There is a limit to how long we can extend our lives.

Thus, it is extremely important to know what death is or, in other words, what happens when we leave this world. Knowing this sooner has a great influence on how we live the rest of our lives.

The majority of people, however, do not know anything other than this world or the world in which their families, friends, coworkers and acquaintances are. For this reason, they want to remain in this world even after death. This gives rise to various troubles and sufferings. When people who have absolutely no knowledge of the spiritual world die, they only know to linger around their families, so their souls wander around in their home. Or, they might visit their friends, grandfathers and grandmothers, or might appear around their coworkers. These souls may remain for years or decades in these areas.

## *Religious professionals are required to have the power Of salvation*

There would not be any problems if the priest conducting a funeral or memorial service knew the Truth. If a priest can accurately explain about the afterlife to the soul of the dead, or to the person's family members and relatives, and can send the soul to Heaven, then the deceased can be saved. However, priests of today do not have this ability.

For example, in order to help people in affected areas after the Great East Japan Earthquake, Buddhist monks opened cafés where they would serve free coffee. It was a nice idea and very kind of them; it may have provided people some comfort and peace of mind. But I would tell them that they must confidently talk about the other world if they are to call themselves monks. Monks must never evade discussions of the other world.

Some priests, both in Buddhism and Christianity, evade discussions of the other world and try to resolve things only by talking about things of this world. But I want to say to them that those who evade these discussions are not worthy to be called religious professionals. They must stand up and face questions such as, "What happens when people die?" "What exactly are God and Buddha doing?" If they are unable to answer these questions, they are not qualified as religious professionals. They must teach people the answers to such questions in a straightforward manner.

Unfortunately, some priests do not know if the other world or soul actually exists, if there is life after death, or why they perform memorial services. Some perform the rituals only because they need to keep their temple alive as a successor. Such attitudes are mistaken; they are not conducting true religious activities. There are probably many such priests, which is not good. A religion is not a religion if it cannot save people in the truest sense. A religion is not authentic unless, upon hearing the teachings, the souls of people who are lost after death can return to where they are supposed to go.

To help people's souls return straight to where they are destined, it is first essential for them to learn and understand the Truth while they are still alive in this world. If that is not possible, the Truth has to be taught to people who are alive now, which is to say the bereaved family members, relatives, friends and others, thereby indirectly communicating the knowledge of the Truth to the souls of the deceased. That is the true memorial service, which will serve to truly console their souls.

Some people may live materialistically without knowing the Truth, or by solely acting under hedonistic thoughts. If such people were to suddenly lose their lives by some natural disaster or accident, they would not have any idea about what happened, where they are, what they should do, and what people around them are doing. For example, if the deceased relatives of the members in the audience come to my lecture as spirits and look down on us from above, they will most likely wonder what is going on, possibly thinking it to be some kind of wedding ceremony.

However, one should not end up like this. This is something that infringes upon human dignity, upon the dignity of the soul. In fact, knowing who you are, knowing how you should live, and furthermore, knowing what you should do after you die are part of what it is to be human, a part of the human condition.

# How to avoid falling into the Asura Realm of Hell
## Or the Hell of Beasts

The power of mercy, the theme of this chapter, is the power of love and the power to care for other people. Having this power is very important in the other world as well because there are many different realms in the other world, and among them are realms that are called Hell.

For example, there is a realm called the Asura Realm, or the Hell of Strife, which is the realm of fighting, destruction, and war. There is also a realm called the Animal Realm, or the Hell of Beasts, where many human souls live like animals and transfigure into animals. In order to avoid going to places like the Asura Realm or the Hell of Beasts, we must have a merciful heart. People with a heart of mercy do not go to those realms.

Figuratively speaking, the realm of fighting and destruction and the realm of animals are realms of "mutual consumption." They are realms where beings consume each other, where they eat each other as food, a realm where inhabitants live in constant fear of losing their life, or in fear of death. They only think of eating other inhabitants. That is why a heart of compassion is essential to avoid going to these kinds of realms.

The reason for this is that compassion allows one to accept and understand the sadness other people hold in their hearts; it is the desire to help others ease their sadness. In other words, if you have a heart of mercy, it means that you already have a head start as a human being.

Conversely, if you cannot comprehend this heart of mercy, then you are basically living in a dog-eat-dog animalistic world or a realm in which people are killed daily, similar to what is currently occurring in the desert regions of the Middle East. That is exactly the same as the Asura Realm, and if you cannot comprehend the heart of mercy, you will return to that kind of world after you die.

I once saw a Tokyo street interview on television of an 11-year-old girl who had come to Japan from an Islamic country. She said she had experienced a missile attack while she was working in the fields with her grandmother, and there were even cases of missiles fired at bridal processions. I was shocked to see that while giving the interview, she kept looking up at the sky, again and again. Apparently, she was so afraid that, even during the interview in Tokyo, she was checking to see if any military drones [unmanned aircraft] were flying above to attack her from the air. That kind of life must be filled with fear.

If people lived with fear and if that is the only world they ever know, after they die they would most probably go to the Asura Realm, a world ruled by fear, because they do not know any other kind of world. Nevertheless, to end after death in a world ruled by fear or a world ruled by the law of the jungle is not a desirable result for humans.

## *Reasons why competition exists in this world*

It is true that there is competition in this world. Depending on the way you look at it, a competitive world may appear like a brutal, animalistic world. However, there is more to humans than simply aiming to win and survive, increasing monetary gain, or having an easy life at the cost of other people or other companies. In that sense, our world is not the same as the world of animals.

Even when you see other companies expanding, it is important that your company continuously aims to create better products to benefit the world. If you want to monopolize sales in a market by crushing other companies, your company will become an animalistic, dog-eat-dog world. Therefore, you must have a heart of mercy. That will create a world where everyone can help and nurture each other.

On the individual level, there is also competition to enter prestigious schools, for example, and some people may harbor ill feelings or jealousy toward people who can study better than they do. On the other hand, those able to study well may scorn, put down, discriminate, or mock people who cannot study, causing all sorts of pain. Such attitudes are due to extreme narrow-mindedness.

Competing just for the sake of competition is wrong. One aspect of competition is that it promotes mutual improvement. If you stay idle and neglect to improve yourself, you are letting down your parents and forgetting the reason you were born.

Do not let your life and your parents' effort go to waste. Instead, strive to study hard and do good work. Aim to be a respectable person who can contribute to society and who can support those in need of help. For this purpose, it is essential to learn a variety of things through friendly rivalry and develop your abilities.

Furthermore, it is important to increase your economic power. Economic power helps you to carve many paths for yourself. Not only can you use it to help yourself, but great economic power serves to help other people as well.

For example, we built Sendai Shoshinkan, hoping it would serve as "a lighthouse of light" and saving many people living in disaster-affected areas from pain and suffering. It cost over a billion yen [over 10 million dollars] to construct it. We could gather such an amount of pure offerings thanks to the donations given by countless people worldwide, and we do not want to let that go to waste. We want that power of funds to become the power to help many people.

## *I want to give the right teachings to As many people as possible*

In this modern era, we are not distributing things like bread or milk. What people want the most are right teachings. "What are human beings?" "Where did we come from, and where do we go?" "What is death?" "What happens when we die?" "If there is suffering after death, how can we be saved from it?" "What can I do to become a wonderful being who can lead people after I die?" Teachings that can answer these fundamental questions are needed now in Japan and across the entire globe.

This is why Happy Science must expand to the next level. We must grow to gain enough power to extend our hands to people around the world. We do not carry out activities merely for our own benefit, profit, or fame.

For example, I gave over 180 lectures in 2014. I, myself, feel that this is an absurd amount. You would be overwhelmed listening to one lecture every two days. Even I feel that way. As I give the lectures, I think to myself that giving 180 lectures a year might kill me and that I might end up dying early. But if I were to die early and leave things untold, I might feel restless, so I continue to give many lectures with the aim of saying all I have to say in as early time as possible.

I am laying down my life for the Truth. I am not just saying this; I am actually putting it into practice. I want to teach the Laws to as many people as possible. I want to give teachings to as many people as possible. I want the heart of love to reach as many people as possible. This concrete action is the very power of mercy.

I want all of you to awaken to this power of mercy dormant in you. Many people are waiting for the Truth. I pray from the bottom of my heart that the light of love will reach all people throughout Japan and the world.

# THE DIFFERENCE BETWEEN TERRORISM AND REVOLUTION

*There have already been enough conflicts between Christianity and Islam.*

*I was involved in the formation of Christianity. I definitely guided Jesus Christ in Judea from Heaven. Over 600 years later, I even guided Muhammad in Saudi Arabia from Heaven. I cannot bear to watch the religions that I engendered continuing to fight each other in hatred for more than 1,000 years.*

*Then, what can we do? We should create a base for a common understanding and preach the teachings. I believe that should be our next goal.*

*Buddhism teaches compassion, salvation and the importance of faith. Much of this philosophy formed the base of Eastern culture and its way of thinking.*

*Mercy is the heart of love that finds in others something you have in yourself. It is to believe*

*in the shining diamond others also have as children of God. It is to believe that the path to enlightenment through effort is open to everyone as a child of Buddha.*

*I believe the only place I can teach this is in Japan, where the West and the East come together. So, I sincerely hope that Japan becomes stronger and that my teachings taught in this country spread to every corner of the world.*

*There is the word, "revolution." It differs from terrorism that some people commit despite believing in a religion of mercy and love. Terrorism and revolution are similar in a way and different in another way. Where does the difference lie?*

*Many terrorists' acts in this world are ruled by vengeance, fury and rage. They want to kill many people for revenge. Nonetheless, I feel that behind these feelings is the belief that God asks for sacrifice. On the other hand, people give many definitions to revolution, but the essence of revolution is to establish freedom. I believe it is completely different*

*from terrorism.*

*Happy Science has been advocating the Happiness Revolution. But our revolution does not use violence. We are seeking to establish freedom in this world by peaceful means. Please understand this difference.*

From *What is the Global Justice that Saves the Earth?*

Chapter SIX

# To the World We Can Believe In

*You, Too, Have the Light*
*To Bring Happiness to the World*

# 1

# Changing the World Through The Revolution of Happiness

✧    ✧    ✧

## *The responsibility and duty as the birthplace of Happy Science teachings*

Looking back over the recent events, the most challenging event for Happy Science was the opening of Happy Science University [HSU] in the spring of 2015. We opened the university despite being disapproved by Japan's Ministry of Education, Culture, Sports, Science and Technology. It was a battle between the state and religion.

I do not think there has ever been a university established without the approval from the ministry. Yet, Happy Science is already an organization that conducts activities in over 100 countries and has formed a large community, so we opened HSU thinking that something approved by El Cantare does not need further approval.

In terms of curriculum content, I felt that we could create a much better learning institution if we stood true to our beliefs. I am not saying that we would not listen to other people's opinions, but degrading the content for the opinions of those with lower awareness would jeopardize the future of our students. Therefore, we decided to move forward without changing the content and by maintaining a high-level curriculum.

This is quite a challenge, but Happy Science is not a religion that would collapse due to mere government oppression. Rather, the government should be concerned about the collapse of the state. Even if the government of Japan falls, Happy Science will not. Even if Japan sinks to the bottom of the sea, our fellow members, active in over 100 countries, have promised to hold up the light of Truth eternally into the future, so we remain confident in ourselves.

Nevertheless, I believe Japan bears great responsibilities and duties as the birthplace of Happy Science teachings. It is important that our activities in Japan move forward as much as possible, because Japan is the pivotal place of El Cantare faith.

In 2015, I published *The Laws of Justice* (New York: IRH Press, 2016) worldwide, which marked my 2,000th book. In addition, I have so far given a total of more than 2,400 lectures [the number of lectures exceeded 2,500 as of November 2016]. Embarrassingly enough, this level is still very far from my ultimate goal and my messages have yet to reach the people of the world, but my aspiration has not waned even a bit since I attained Great Enlightenment 35 years ago, founded Happy Science 30 years ago, and since we became a religious institution 25 years ago. We cannot feel content or satisfied at this level.

You will understand what I mean if you look at the teachings that I have been giving from the very beginning. The teachings contain the creation of the universe. Do you think it is acceptable for a religion that gives the teachings on Creation to only be acknowledged as one of tens of thousands of religions in Japan? Absolutely not. Certainly, Happy Science has grown into a large religious organization after having been born in Japan in the postwar era and has attained a level to gain a place in the world, but we cannot allow ourselves to stay at this level.

The year 2016 marked the 35th year since my Great Enlightenment and 30th year since the founding of Happy Science. What is more, according to one type of calendar, 2016 is said to be a year of revolution. [The philosophy of yin yang and the Five Agents or Elements (Metal, Wood, Water, Fire and Earth) in Chinese cosmology says that 2016 is the year of the Fire Monkey that comes around once every 60 years, and is believed to be a year of revolution.] This being so, who will start the revolution, if not us?

The time has come for us to use the strength we have accumulated as a group for 30 years, and turn the Dharma Wheel further and stronger in Japan and the world to let people know of our existence.

## *Happy Science has been granted the authority to Change this world by the heavenly world far above*

People who read Happy Science teachings as mere writings in print may take them as knowledge they can use in their own lives. However, if you openheartedly accept the teachings as they are written, you will see that all religions—including Judaism, Christianity, Buddhism, Islam and Japanese Shinto—will be absorbed into the

Happy Science movement. They are teachings of extremely grand scale. And I feel that the time to prove whether this is true or not is drawing closer.

We are definitely not doing this activity for the sake of gaining power or reputation. We are not doing it to seek respect from many people. We are trying to start a revolution, not a violent one, but a happiness revolution. Only after we have brought happiness to many people, can we say we have changed the world and made it a better place.

Happy Science is currently taking on challenges in various fields. We have yet to see the desired results in any of these fields. But eventually, the day will come when most of humanity will understand the significance of today. If people in the world realize and accept who is giving this lecture at Makuhari Messe in Japan and to whom this lecture is directed, even the pope would have to take off his crown and give his respect. I make it clear that we have attained this stage.

Happy Science might not yet have the power to change the world. However, we have been granted the authority to change the world. This authority was given from a far and distant world above this earthly world.

The Book of Genesis in the Old Testament says that God separated Heaven and Earth. The name of the God is "El," the "El" in El Cantare. Many of the people in the world do not understand what this really means. But as more time passes, more people will come to truly understand its greatness.

# 2

# To Live in the World We Can Believe In

✧　　✧　　✧

### *The laws of a Being who has been guiding humanity From the very beginning of Creation*

I published *The Laws of Justice* as my laws series for 2016. The book served as the North Star, the power to guide the country of Japan from 2016 onward. Is there anyone else who can now preach the Laws of Justice in the world? Can the prime minister of Japan preach the Laws of Justice? Can the chief justice of the Supreme Court or the secretary-general of the United Nations preach these laws? How about the pope or Dalai Lama? Who can preach them?

There is only one person who can. I am preaching what the world needs right now. What the world presently needs are teachings about what is right. These cannot be taught from years of accumulated academic studies of this world or experience through secular jobs. They can only be taught by a Being that has been guiding humanity from the distant heavenly world for several thousands, tens of thousands of years or even longer. Those are the laws I am preaching. I am not trying to be conceited; I am stating the truth.

In the world today, much confusion occurs between religions, some of them appearing to be religious wars. In other places, there are also battles between religion and atheism or materialism.

There has never been a time more important than now to teach what the truth is. Although I do not necessarily approve of conflict and war, if they rise due to people's ignorance of what is right, then I believe it is my job to teach it.

Just imagine that a Being, who has been guiding humankind since the beginning of the heavens and the earth, is showing people how to think about the problems of the world and the direction of the future. If everyone is able to agree with and accept that guidance, then the mundane and frivolous conflicts would all disappear from the earth.

Now is the time to show people the spiritual significance of the power of enlightenment. The power of enlightenment goes beyond the righteousness of academic studies and research of this world. It surpasses scientific and journalistic methods or the modern principles of righteousness, which determine the truth by seeing what remains after removing all suspicion and doubt. We must tell people that there is such a higher level of righteousness.

In this regard, this message is not addressed only to the audiences who attended my lecture on site or through broadcast via satellite on that day; they are not the only ones who need to understand the content of my lecture. This chapter, "To the World We Can Believe In," was originally a lecture given in Japanese and was translated into different languages and broadcast worldwide to hundreds of locations with some time difference, but it should essentially have been done in English, considering its content. Nevertheless, I decided to give it in Japanese because Japanese followers have extremely important work to do.

## *We should not judge everything*
## *Based solely on worldly perspective*

It is important to explain why the Laws of Justice is needed. The reason why I am preaching the Laws of Justice now is to build the world we can believe in. We have the right to live in a world that we can believe more in; it would be very sad if we can only believe in what can be seen, touched or have to do with our physical body.

In addition, there are many groups that take the form of a religion, but have forgotten their true mission. For example, a very difficult problem lies in the conflicts involving Islam. Perhaps, the majority of the world hopes that air strikes by the developed countries will end the war. However, although they are Christian countries, they are not following the teachings of Christ. They are attacking Muslim countries based on the rules that humans made in this world. The people being attacked, on the other hand, are believers of Islam. Bombs and missiles are falling on people who are praying to Allah.

How does God see this? Humans on earth should consider this point.

To find the answer to this question, we must not judge everything based solely on worldly perspective. The perspective of the other world is the value that has almost been lost in many religions around the world. This is because the world has become much too convenient and affluent. As a result, even in Christian countries, heavier emphasis is being placed on materialistic inventions, science, practical studies and work theory, and faith is being relegated only to churches.

## *Religions are limited by the time and place In which they were founded*

Islam continues to engage in primitive ways of fighting, shedding much blood just as the founder Muhammad and his successors did in establishing the religion. What is their purpose? We need to reconsider this.

Indeed, there is much fighting in the history of religion. Many battles were fought when Moses led the Exodus to eventually reach Canaan. Much blood was shed during the times when Jesus conducted his activities centered around what is now Israel. Rome also experienced many wars. Islam was founded 600 years after Christianity, and at that time, too, many battles were fought among the different clans and tribes within the same religion. When a new religion was founded, older gods were destroyed. Many events occurred in this way, and if you look only at this fighting from a worldly perspective, it is understandable that some people think they would be much happier not believing in a religion.

However, I daresay unto you. These religions were taught in the ancient times of 3,000, 2,500, 2,000, and 1,400 years ago. Undoubtedly, there were people who were able to hear the voice of God, but they heard it from their own standpoint. This is something that people should bear in mind.

As a prophet or messiah of a country or a tribe, each of them heard the teachings of God and spread those from their own position, for the good of their own people. For this reason, religions founded by them were limited by the age and location in which they were active.

Misunderstandings arose as the world became more closely connected, with frequent travel and communication reaching the other side of the globe. People cannot imagine that God had given teachings solely for their own tribe, people or ethnic group. Therefore, many people misinterpret the phrases, "You shall have no other Gods before me," or "Believe only in our tribe's God" to mean, "The God that leads our tribe or ethnic group is the only true God, so deny all other gods because they are wrong."

## The devil's thinking is obstructing The future of Thailand

We must consider the era and region in which each religion was taught. For example, Shakyamuni Buddha spread his teachings in India 2,500 or 2,600 years ago. He was born in what is now Nepal, and his work centered on the middle reaches of the Ganges River in India. His missionary activities were within walking distance, so while he was alive, his group of followers only grew to a medium-sized level in terms of that era. He did train his disciples and send them to various other places, but it was not known what became of them or their missionary activities; this is how Buddhist diffusion was at that time.

Over 2,000 years had passed, and a part of the Buddha's teachings had come to Japan in the form of Mahayana Buddhism. Unfortunately, however, the original teachings of Shakyamuni Buddha have been lost, and it has become like an empty shell.

On the other hand, countries such as Sri Lanka and Thailand adhere to Theravada Buddhism, which is said to faithfully follow the original teachings of the Buddha. Thailand, in particular, has always kept its independence, so its religious tradition has been strictly preserved.

In the past, I had planned to go to Thailand twice for lectures, but unfortunately, I could not go on either attempt. [The lectures were scheduled to be held in September 2011, and in November 2013, but both were canceled due to reasons connected to the Spirit World of Thailand. For more details, refer to *Hikaku Shukyo Gaku kara Mita Kofuku no Kagaku Gaku Nyumon* (literally, "Introduction to the Study of Happy Science from the Perspective of Comparative Religion") (Tokyo: IRH Press, 2014).] My books have been translated into Thai, too, but the people there are saying that they cannot accept *The Rebirth of Buddha*.

There are three seals, or basic tenets, in Buddhism called the "impermanence of all things," the "egolessness of all phenomena" and the "perfect tranquility of nirvana." Theravada Buddhism teaches the last one, the "perfect tranquility of nirvana," to mean that the Buddha will never come back to this world again once he attains enlightenment and becomes free from any earthly bondage and returns to Nirvana. This is why the Thai people are saying that they cannot accept the concept of the rebirth of Buddha.

Sri Lanka is another country of Theravada Buddhism, and when I went there to give a lecture, I asked the audience to think about who would be happy with the Buddha not returning to this world. I said, "Suppose the Buddha never came back to this world after attaining enlightenment. It means he would no longer guide the people on earth. Who would be happy with this? The devil, of course. Who is the one that interpreted the Buddha's teachings like that? Think hard about this."

Then, more than 9,000 out of 13,000 people who had attended my lecture became members of Happy Science [see, *Okawa Ryuho, Sri Lanka Junshaku no Kiseki* (literally, "Ryuho Okawa's Missionary Tour Footsteps in Sri Lanka") (Tokyo: IRH Press, 2012)]. This was because I pointed out to them that it is the devil who wishes that the Buddha does not return to this world.

By attaining enlightenment, you will be set free from any attachments. This is indeed the Truth taught by the Buddha. Once you return to the spiritual world, you will be completely free, liberated from all physical bondage and restraints. Your thoughts become all there is, and what you decide become your actions. The Buddha preached that this complete freedom is the state of enlightenment.

However, if people believe the Buddha attaining Nirvana means being confined inside a cave, somewhere in dark mountains, just remaining still, that is truly an embarrassing misunderstanding. That in no way is the truth. If it were, it would be the same as the Buddha being in a deep cave in Hell. If the Buddha cannot leave the state of Nirvana to save people on earth who are seeking salvation, this is not enlightenment. This is nonsense; it is the same as materialism and a mistaken theory of religion. The future will hardly open for Thailand unless they break through this.

# 3

# Faith is Something You Embrace And Feel with All Your Heart and Soul

✧　✧　✧

## Battles against materialism and Atheism in the field of academic studies

In Chapter One of *The Laws of Justice*, I mentioned the American movie, *God's Not Dead*, which was released in 2014. The movie depicts the following event at a university in the United States, a Christian country. There is a course in which all students are asked to sign a paper stating they do not believe in God and unless they signed it, they would fail the course, which would affect their grades and would further affect their becoming successful in society. But a Christian student refuses to write, "God is dead." From there, he begins a debate with the professor. This is the movie storyline, but it most probably reflects the current state of academics in America.

In the field of science, in particular, there are many cases where the teachings of Christianity are completely overturned. For example, Professor Stephen Hawking, theoretical physicist and cosmologist, denies God. He says he cannot believe that God created the universe. Evolutionary biologist Richard Dawkins says that the true nature of the soul is DNA. He says that DNA replicates and transfers from parents to children, and children to grandchildren, and that this cycle of DNA itself is the reincarnation of the soul. These statements are so foolish and ridiculous, but at universities, unless you believe in these and write your answers according to them, you will not be able to graduate as a top student or get a good job. Even in a Christian country, this is becoming mainstream, and that is why there are battles happening everywhere.

In fact, professors tell the students that while it is fine to believe in God in church or at home, faith should be excluded from the university class because there is no proof. And, in order to teach agnosticism or atheism, they ask the students to sign a paper denying God. Since the majority of philosophers today are atheists, they need to have their students deny God in order to teach their ideologies. That is why they even ask them to sign such a statement.

However, even if students were to get A's in this way and proceed with their higher education, get a good job, have a good marriage and build a decent family, could they ultimately be happy by denying God? Can they truly be happy by living in ways that go against the Truth? Do you really think you deserve respect or are praiseworthy by being arrogant enough to deny God? Is life, scientific knowledge, or academic study based on such thoughts respectable? Even if this was conducted in the world's top-class, most prestigious university, what is wrong is wrong. A lie is a lie. I am saying that there is a limit to how far we can go on teaching things that should not be taught.

## Everything unfolds in the grand palm Of God and Buddha

It is not that faith is behind and education is advanced. Academic studies use only parts of our brain, but faith is something we embrace and feel with all our heart and soul. It is taken in and felt by all our physical senses, soul, and the entire spirit. That is faith. And that is why faith is sacred. Faith incorporates academic studies within it; it is not one of the subjects of academic studies.

It is a big mistake to believe that religion is a mere practical activity researched by religious studies, one tiny field among numerous academic fields. Everything exists and is active on the grand palm of God and Buddha.

Faith encompasses everything, including the Earth, the Solar System, the Milky Way Galaxy and the countless number of other galaxies that exist far beyond, the many civilizations rising and falling in those galaxies and all animate things living there, as well as what they create and think about. This Truth includes matters of difficult content far surpassing the teachings on the existence of the spiritual world.

At Happy Science, we have been conducting space-people readings and receiving spiritual messages of various space people [refer to Ryuho Okawa, *Uchu no Ho Nyumon* (literally, "Introduction to the Laws of the Universe") (Tokyo: IRH Press, 2010) and *Uchujin Reading* (literally, "Space-People Reading") (Tokyo: IRH Press)]. Some of these include histories of hundreds of millions of years ago, or what the extraterrestrial beings had experienced before coming to Earth. Therefore, although some of these readings have been made public, the parts that are seemingly difficult for the general public to understand have only been made available as books or videos for internal study material for our members.

I am sure that these will be the first textbooks that future societies will use to learn about space. It is extremely difficult to unveil the mysticism of the great universe as long as we remain at a level where we have to use a space shuttle for space travel. That is why I am giving teachings that trace back to the creation of the universe. It might take 50 to 100 years to prove even a part of what I teach; it would probably take more than 1,000 years to prove everything. But I am now teaching the laws that need to be left for people who will live more than 1,000 years in the future.

Naturally, there may be parts that contemporary people are unable to fully comprehend. But there definitely must be certain areas that you understand and that resonate with you. If so, please be aware that my teachings include elements that are very important for people in the future, even if they are beyond the understanding of contemporary generations. I hope you wish strongly in your heart that these teachings will be passed down very carefully for the sake of future generations.

# 4

# Your Ultimate Goal is to Completely Believe in God

## *Right now, God that has been guiding humankind is Alive on earth*

Looking throughout the world now, there is no religion as active as Happy Science. Not only is it active, but in terms of content, it has surpassed that of the Genesis in the Bible and the ancient religions of Mesopotamia. Our teachings have also revealed far older history than what is told by the old allegories of Buddhism, the religions of ancient Egypt, and Greek mythology. Our teachings have indicated the distant future of humankind as well. Our guiding compass does not point at something small just in front of us.

Of course, I am also thankful for the advancement in civilization, which made possible the broadcast of my lecture from Japan to the world. In such an advanced age, we must make miracles greater than the ones that occurred during the time of Moses, Buddha, Jesus

Christ or Muhammad happen.

I have given lectures on various themes, big and small, for 35 years since attaining enlightenment. And you, too, have arrived at a point where you need to start on your true mission. You cannot stop at just having your own faith. The stage of just being active inside a small organization is over. From now onward, we must act by believing that we bear responsibility for the world.

In doing so, it is vital to shift this world from "the world we cannot believe in" to "the world we can believe in," as the title of this chapter states. From the viewpoint of modern medical scientists, most religious teachings may well be put into "the world we cannot believe in." Medically speaking, illness will not be cured, humans all die or get ill, and miracles do not happen. This is the commonly accepted view in medical textbooks.

However, despite this common knowledge, a lot of miracles are happening, even now, in the environment surrounding Happy Science. For example, many miracles have happened, such as the healing of intractable, rare, or terminal diseases after attending my lectures. Similar things also happened to people listening to my lectures over satellite broadcasting. There are even reports of physical ailments improving just by receiving a flyer of my lecture, or by simply watching a Happy Science movie.

These examples show how great the power is that is now working behind us. God is not dead. God is alive. He is alive, and is working now. He has appeared in front of you and is guiding you. The one standing before you is a human named Ryuho Okawa but please know that this is one aspect of God.

## *The most sacred love is the love to spread the Truth*

No matter what kinds of oppression I may face, I have absolutely no intention of bending my conviction or surrendering. The Truth is the Truth, what is good is good, and what is right is right. If commonly accepted knowledge is wrong, then we will crush it.

When are we going to do this? This year? Next year? In five years? In ten years? After we die? There is no time to even think about when. Each and every person must shine the torch within his or her mind. You have the mission of advancing into the dark night with that torch.

Everyone is given light. The light you have received from me is surely lit within you. With that light as your guide, move forward wholeheartedly into the dark night. There will be no end to your work until you light up all the darkness around the world. Please do not forget the message you heard on this day, at this moment, on this night.

I will be here with you on earth for a while, light up this world and turn the Dharma Wheel. The laws I preach are Eternal Laws that must not perish after 500 years, 1,000 years, 2,000 years and even 3,000 years. As someone who listened to these Eternal Laws, please engrave them with pride in your heart, and carve a path through your daily life.

And tell about the Truth you understood to the people around you, to the people you can reach, to the people who can hear your voice. Tell them as much as you can. That is love.

The most sacred love between people is the love to convey the Truth. To tell people about the Truth is the most sacred love.

In the world, there are certainly people who are starving, suffering from illness, or going through many hardships. However, just because suffering, hardship, and adversity occurs in this world does not mean God does not exist. God is needed because there are so many people living in these kinds of misfortune.

And God does exist. Please return to your starting point and begin by believing. Your starting point is to believe. And your ultimate goal is to completely believe in God. Begin by having faith, and end by fully believing.

What does it mean to have full faith in this world? Show it in your thoughts, words and actions. This is what I ask of you in this chapter.

# EVERYTHING BECOMES LIGHT WHEN WE BREAK THROUGH WALLS

*Our battle will not end*
*Until we establish God's justice*
*And build a true Religious Nation.*
*The young generation*
*That will lead*
*The 21st century,*
*Please follow us!*
*We have high expectations of you.*
*We will break through the walls soon.*

When excavating a mountain,
We need to bore a tunnel.
During the construction,
Those who are digging the tunnel do not know
Whether their work is producing any value.
It may seem they are wasting their time.

However, once the tunnel comes through
The other side of the mountain,
All the efforts that seemed a waste
Become a shining light.

From *What is the Justice that Saves the Earth?*

# AFTERWORD

*The Laws of Mission* is "the Laws of Miracles"
To live through the age of the mind.
These laws are founded on wisdom
And overflow with mercy.
Oh, how hard it is
To tell people whose eyes can see,
"You are not seeing the world of truth."
Oh, how hard it is
To say, "Take a leap"
To people who believe
That constant skepticism is what brings them to the truth.

Oh, how hard it is
To speak about the world of ideas and the world of faith
To people who believe
That only what can be scientifically proved
Are genuine academic studies.
Oh, how hard it is
To speak of and spread the fact
That I am the Savior.

*Ryuho Okawa*
*Founder and CEO of Happy Science Group*
*December 2016*

*This book is a compilation of the lectures,
with additions, as listed below.*

- Chapter 1 -

## Living in the Age of the Mind

Lecture given on June 7, 2015
at Tachikawa Local Temple, Tokyo, Japan

- Chapter 2 -

## How to Become an Attractive Person

Lecture given on April 28, 2013
at Tokyo Shoshinkan, Tokyo, Japan

- Chapter 3 -

## The Starting Point for Human Happiness

Lecture given on April 23, 2016
at ASTY Tokushima, Tokushima, Japan

- Chapter 4 -

## The Power of Miracles to Change the Era

Lecture given on March 13, 2016
at Marine Messe Fukuoka, Fukuoka, Japan

- Chapter 5 -

## Awakening to the Power of Mercy

Lecture given on November 21, 2015
at Sendai Shoshinkan, Miyagi, Japan

- Chapter 6 -

## To the World We Can Believe In

Lecture given on December 15, 2015
at Makuhari Messe, Chiba, Japan

* *Contemplative Quotes* are taken from other books by the author.

# ABOUT THE AUTHOR

RYUHO OKAWA is global visionary, renowned spiritual leader, and internationally best-selling author with a simple goal: to help people find true happiness and create a better world.

His deep compassion and sense of responsibility for the happiness of each individual has prompted him to publish over 2,200 titles of religious, spiritual, and self-development teachings, covering a broad range of topics including how our thoughts influence reality, the nature of love, and the path to enlightenment. He also writes on the topics of management and economy, as well as the relationship between religion and politics in the global context. To date, Okawa's books have sold over 100 million copies worldwide and been translated into 28 languages.

Okawa has dedicated himself to improving society and creating a better world. In 1986, Okawa founded Happy Science as a spiritual movement dedicated to bringing greater happiness to humankind by uniting religions and cultures to live in harmony. Happy Science has grown rapidly from its beginnings in Japan to a worldwide organization with over twelve million members. Okawa is compassionately committed to the spiritual growth of others. In addition to writing and publishing books, he continues to give lectures around the world.

# WHAT IS A SPIRITUAL MESSAGE?

We are all spiritual beings living on this earth. The following is the mechanism behind Ryuho Okawa's spiritual messages.

## 1 You are a spirit

People are born into this world to gain wisdom through various experiences and return to the other world when their lives end. We are all spirits and repeat this cycle in order to refine our souls.

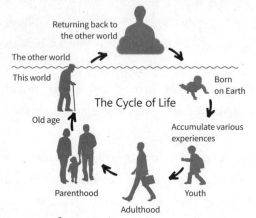

## 2 You have a guardian spirit

Guardian spirits are those who protect the people living on this earth. Each of us has a guardian spirit that watches over us and guides us from the other world. They are one of our past lives, and are identical in how we think.

## 3 How spiritual messages work

Since guardian spirits think at the same subconscious level as the person living on earth, Ryuho Okawa can summon the spirit and find out what the person on earth is actually thinking. If the person has already returned to the other world, the spirit can give messages to the people living on earth through Ryuho Okawa.

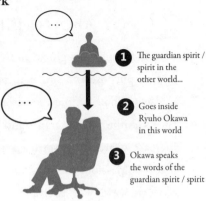

1 The guardian spirit / spirit in the other world...

2 Goes inside Ryuho Okawa in this world

3 Okawa speaks the words of the guardian spirit / spirit

The spiritual messages of more than 700 sessions have been openly recorded by Ryuho Okawa since 2009, and the majority of these have been published. Spiritual messages from the guardian spirits of living politicians such as U.S. President Trump, Japanese Prime Minister Shinzo Abe and Chinese President Xi Jinping, as well as spiritual messages sent from the Spirit World by Jesus Christ, Muhammad, Thomas Edison, Mother Teresa, Steve Jobs and Nelson Mandela are just a tiny pack of spiritual messages that were published so far.

Domestically, in Japan, these spiritual messages are being read by a wide range of politicians and mass media, and the high-level contents of these books are delivering an impact even more on politics, news and public opinion. In recent years, there have been spiritual messages recorded in English, and English translations are being done on the spiritual messages given in Japanese. These have been published overseas, one after another, and have started to shake the world.

*For more about spiritual messages and a complete list of books, visit okawabooks.com*

# ABOUT HAPPY SCIENCE

Happy Science is a global movement that empowers individuals to find purpose and spiritual happiness and to share that happiness with their families, societies, and the world. With more than twelve million members around the world, Happy Science aims to increase awareness of spiritual truths and expand our capacity for love, compassion, and joy so that together we can create the kind of world we all wish to live in.

Activities at Happy Science are based on the Principles of Happiness (Love, Wisdom, Self-Reflection, and Progress). These principles embrace worldwide philosophies and beliefs, transcending boundaries of culture and religions.

Love teaches us to give ourselves freely without expecting anything in return; it encompasses giving, nurturing, and forgiveness.

Wisdom leads us to the insights of spiritual truths, and opens us to the true meaning of life and the will of God (the universe, the highest power, Buddha).

Self-Reflection brings a mindful, nonjudgmental lens to our thoughts and actions to help us find our truest selves—the essence of our souls—and deepen our connection to the highest power. It helps us attain a clean and peaceful mind and leads us to the right life path.

Progress emphasizes the positive, dynamic aspects of our spiritual growth—actions we can take to manifest and spread happiness around the world. It's a path that not only expands our soul growth, but also furthers the collective potential of the world we live in.

# Programs and Events

The doors of Happy Science are open to all. We offer a variety of programs and events, including self-exploration and self-growth programs, spiritual seminars, meditation and contemplation sessions, study groups, and book events.

*Our programs are designed to:*

- Deepen your understanding of your purpose and meaning in life
- Improve your relationships and increase your capacity to love unconditionally
- Attain a peace of mind, decrease anxiety and stress, and feel positive
- Gain deeper insights and broader perspective on the world
- Learn how to overcome life's challenges
  ... and much more.

For more information, visit happyscience-na.org or happy-science.org

# International Seminars

Each year, friends from all over the world join our international seminars, held at our faith centers in Japan. Different programs are offered each year and cover a wide variety of topics, including improving relationships, practicing the Eightfold Path to enlightenment, and loving yourself, to name just a few.

# Happy Science Monthly

Our monthly publication covers the latest featured lectures, members' life-changing experiences and other news from members around the world, book reviews, and many other topics. Downloadable PDF files are available at happyscience-na.org. Copies and back issues in Portuguese, Chinese, and other languages are available upon request. For more information, contact us via e-mail at tokyo@happy-science.org.

# CONTACT INFORMATION

Happy Science is a worldwide organization with faith centers around the globe. For a comprehensive list of centers, visit the worldwide directory at happy-science.org or happyscience-na.org. The following are some of the many Happy Science locations:

## UNITED STATES AND CANADA

**New York**
79 Franklin Street
New York, NY 10013
Phone: 212-343-7972
Fax: 212-343-7973
Email: ny@happy-science.org
Website: newyork.happyscience-na.org

**New Jersey**
725 River Rd. #102B
Edgewater, NJ 07020
Phone: 201-313-0127
Fax: 201-313-0120
Email: nj@happy-science.org
Website: newjersey.happyscience-na.org

**San Francisco**
525 Clinton Street
Redwood City, CA 94062
Phone&Fax: 650-363-2777
Email: sf@happy-science.org
Website: sanfrancisco.happy
science-na.org

**Atlanta**
1874 Piedmont Ave.
NE Suite 360-C
Atlanta, GA 30324
Phone: 404-892-7770
Email: atlanta@happy-science.org
Website: atlanta.happyscience-na.org

**Florida**
5208 8th St. Zephyrhills, FL 33542
Phone: 813-715-0000
Fax: 813-715-0010
Email: florida@happy-science.org
Website: florida.happyscience-na.org

**Los Angeles**
1590 E. Del Mar Blvd.
Pasadena, CA 91106
Phone: 626-395-7775
Fax: 626-395-7776
Email: la@happy-science.org
Website: losangeles.happyscience-na.org

**Orange County**
10231 Slater Ave #204
Fountain Valley, CA 92708
Phone: 714-745-1140
Email: oc@happy-science.org


**San Diego**
7841 Balboa Ave
Suite #202
San Diego, CA 92111
Phone: 619-381-7615
Fax: 626-395-7776
Email: sandiego@happy-science.org
Website: happyscience-la.org


**Hawaii**
1221 Kapiolani Blvd. Suite 920,
Honolulu HI 96814
Phone: 808-591-9772
Fax: 808-591-9776
Email: hi@happy-science.org
Website: hawaii.happyscience-na.org

**Kauai**
4504 Kukui Street
Dragon Building Suite 21
Kapaa, HI 96746
Phone: 808-822-7007
Fax: 808-822-6007
Email: kauai-hi@happy-science.org
Website: kauai.happyscience-na.org


**Toronto**
845 The Queensway Etobicoke,
ON M8Z 1N6 Canada
Phone: 1-416-901-3747
Email: toronto@happy-science.org
Website: happy-science.ca


**Vancouver**
#212-2609 East 49th Avenue Vancouver,
BC,V5S 1J9 Canada
Phone: 1-604-437-7735
Fax: 1-604-437-7764
Email: vancouver@happy-science.org
Website: happy-science.ca


# INTERNATIONAL

**Tokyo**
1-6-7 Togoshi, Shinagawa
Tokyo, 142-0041 Japan
Phone: 81-3-6384-5770
Fax: 81-3-6384-5776
Email: tokyo@happy-science.org
Website: happy-science.org

**London**
3 Margaret Street
London, W1W 8RE
United Kingdom
Phone: 44-20-7323-9255
Fax: 44-20-7323-9344
Email: eu@happy-science.org
Website: happyscience-uk.org

**Sydney**

516 Pacific Hwy Lane Cove North,
NSW 2066 Australia
Phone: 61-2-9411-2877
Fax: 61-2-9411-2822
Email: sydney@happy-science.org

**Brazil Headquarters**

Rua. Domingos de Morais 1154, Vila
Mariana, Sao Paulo,
CEP 04009-002 Brazil
Phone: 55-11-5088-3800
Fax: 55-11-5088-3806
Email: sp@happy-science.org
Website: cienciadafelicidade.com.br

**Jundiai**

Rua Congo, 447, Jd. Bonfiglioli
Jundiai, CEP 13207-340
Phone: 55-11-4587-5952
Email: jundiai@happy-sciece.org

**Seoul**

74, Sadang-ro 27-gil,
Dongjak-gu, Seoul, Korea
Phone: 82-2-3478-8777
Fax: 82-2- 3478-9777
Email: korea@happy-science.org

Website: happyscience-korea.org

**Taipei**

No. 89, Lane 155, Dunhua N. Road
Songshan District, Taipei City 105 Taiwan
Phone: 886-2-2719-9377
Fax: 886-2-2719-5570
Email: taiwan@happy-science.org
Website: happyscience-tw.org

**Malaysia**

No 22A, Block2, Jalil Link, Jalan
Jalil Jaya 2, Bukit Jalil 57000
Kuala Lumpur Malaysia
Phone: 60-3-8998-7877
Fax: 60-3-8998-7977
Email: Malaysia@happy-science.org
Website: happyscience.org.my

**Nepal**

Kathmandu Metropolitan City
Ward No. 15, Ring Road,
Kimdol, Sitapaila,
Kathmandu, Nepal
Phone: 977-1-427-2931
Email: nepal@happy-science.org

**Uganda**

Plot 877 Rubaga Road,
Kampala P.O. Box 34130
Kampala, Uganda
Phone: 256-79-3238-002
Email: uganda@happy-science.org
Website: happyscience-uganda.org

## About IRH Press USA

IRH Press USA Inc. was founded in 2013 as an affiliated firm of IRH Press Co., Ltd. Based in New York, the press publishes books in various categories including spirituality, religion, and self-improvement and publishes books by Ryuho Okawa, the author of 100 million books sold worldwide. For more information, visit OkawaBooks.com.

Follow us on:
Facebook: Okawa Books
Twitter: Okawa Books
Goodreads: Ryuho Okawa
Instagram: OkawaBooks
Pinterest: Okawa Books

# BOOKS BY RYUHO OKAWA

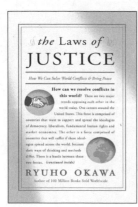

## THE LAWS OF JUSTICE

How We Can Solve World Conflicts & Bring Peace

Softcover • 208 pages • $15.95
• ISBN: 978-1-942125-05-1

This book shows what global justice is from a comprehensive perspective of the Supreme God. Becoming aware of this view will let us embrace differences in beliefs, recognize other peoples divine nature, and love and forgive one another. It will also become the key to solving the issues we face, whether they're religious, political, societal, economic, or academic, and help the world become a better and safer world for all of us living today.

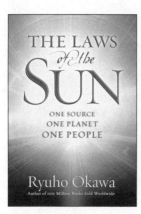

## THE LAWS OF THE SUN

One Source, One Planet, One People

Hardcover • 264 pages • $24.95
• ISBN: 978-1-937673-04-8

Imagine if you could ask God why He created this world and what spiritual laws He used to shape us—and everything around us. In *The Laws of the Sun*, Okawa outlines these laws of the universe and provides a road map for living one's life with greater purpose and meaning. This powerful book shows the way to realize true happiness—a happiness that continues from this world through the other.

## THE LAWS OF SUCCESS

A Spiritual Guide to Turning Your Hopes Into Reality

Softcover • 208 pages • $15.95
• ISBN: 978-1-942125-15-0

The Laws of Success offers 8 spiritual principles that, when put to practice in our day-to-day life, will help us attain lasting success and let us experience the fulfillment of living our purpose and the joy of sharing our happiness with many others. The timeless wisdom and practical steps that Okawa offers will guide us through any difficulties and problems we may face in life, and serve as guiding principles for living a positive, constructive, and meaningful life.

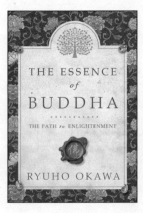

## THE ESSENCE OF BUDDHA

The Path to Enlightenment

Softcover • 208pages • $14.95
• ISBN: 978-1-942125-06-8

By offering a new perspective on core Buddhist thoughts that have long been cloaked in mystique, Okawa brings these teachings to life for modern people. *The Essence of Buddha* distills a way of life that anyone can practice to achieve a life of self-growth, compassionate living, and true happiness.

## A LIFE OF TRIUMPH

Unleashing Your Light Upon the World

Softcover • 240 pages • $15.95
• ISBN: 978-942125-11-2

There is a power within you that can lift your heart from despair to hope, from hardship to happiness, and from defeat to triumph. In this book, Okawa explains the key attitudes that will help you continuously tap the everlasting reserves of positivity, courage, and energy that are already a part of you so you can realize your dreams and become a wellspring of happiness. You'll also find many inspirational poems and a contemplation exercise to inspirit your inner light in times of adversity and in your day-to-day life.

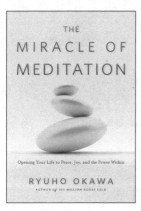

## THE MIRACLE OF MEDITATION

Opening Your Life to Peace, Joy, and the Power Within

Softcover • 208pages • $15.95
• ISBN: 978-1-942125-09-9

Meditation can open your mind to the self-transformative potential within and connect your soul to the wisdom of heaven-all through the power of belief. This book combines the power of faith and the practice of meditation to help you create inner Peace, discover your inner divinity, become your ideal self, and cultivate a purposeful life of altruism and compassion.

# LIST OF OTHER BOOKS BY RYUHO OKAWA

## LAW SERIES

### THE LAWS OF SUCCESS
A Spiritual Guide to Turning Your Hopes Into Reality

### THE LAWS OF JUSTICE
How We Can Solve World Conflicts & Bring Peace

### THE LAWS OF THE SUN
One Source, One Planet, One People

### THE NINE DIMENSIONS
Unveiling the Laws of Eternity

## OTHERS

### HEALING FROM WITHIN
Life-Changing Keys to Calm, Spiritual, and Healthy Living

### THE UNHAPPINESS SYNDROME
28 Habits of Unhappy People (and How to Change Them)

### INVITATION TO HAPPINESS
7 Inspirations from Your Inner Angel

### MESSAGES FROM HEAVEN
What Jesus, Buddha, Moses, and Muhammad Would Say Today

### THINK BIG!
Be Positive and Be Brave to Achieve Your Dreams

### THE HEART OF WORK
10 Keys to Living Your Calling

### THE TRUMP SECRET
Seeing Through the Past, Present, and Future of the New American President

For a complete list of books, visit OkawaBooks.com.